T0064296

TALK TO THE LORD,
and
HE WILL LISTEN

A Study of Prayer

DOROTHY LACROIX

WESTBOW®
PRESS
A DIVISION OF THOMAS NELSON
& ZONDERVAN

New Revised Standard Version Bible, copyright 1989, Division of
Christian Education of the National Council of the Churches of Christ
in the United States of America. Used by permission. All rights reserved.

WestBow Press books may be ordered through
booksellers or by contacting:

WestBow Press
A Division of Thomas Nelson & Zondervan
1663 Liberty Drive
Bloomington, IN 47403
www.westbowpress.com
1 (866) 928-1240

ISBN: 978-1-4908-3660-7 (sc)
ISBN: 978-1-4908-3661-4 (e)

Library of Congress Control Number: 2014908346

Printed in the United States of America.

WestBow Press rev. date: 5/19/2014

SPEAK UP, HE IS LISTENING; He is waiting, waiting to hear from you. How long has it been since you spoke to him? He waits patiently to hear from you. He longs for the sound of your voice.

He longs for your presence. His arms are stretched wide, waiting to gather you close to His loving heart. In John 14:2, Jesus tells his disciples that the Father's home has many rooms. God yearns to welcome you to His home. Here you can find strength, find wisdom, and find peace. God yearns to hear from you, to feel your presence as you draw near in prayer.

So, why a book on prayer? Why is it so detailed that it takes a whole book for an explanation? Perhaps we should take a good look at that little 3 letter word "why", it is used over and over in our lives. It first appears in early childhood; mama and dada are shortly followed by "no" and then quickly followed by "why". No matter what parents are telling a small child, the child will invariably ask "why". For a while a simple answer like, "because I say so" will suffice. But in time an actual response will be required.

As we become adults the "whys" do not cease; if anything they appear more and more frequently. The word "why" is a big part of our daily lives. By now I am sure another 'why' has appeared. You are wondering why I would spend time and space on a little three letter word; wondering what does this little word have to do with a book on prayer.

Often our "why" does not have an apparent answer, sometimes it is more of an expressed thought than an actual question. However, this "why" does have an answer. The answer has several parts which will be covered in ensuing chapters. The part I am sure is first in your minds is "Why a whole book on prayer?" This is the part I will cover now since the other parts could lose impact without it.

I have moved a number of times, finally to a little town in Wisconsin to be nearer to my elderly mother. Very shortly I became a member of a church and quickly became very active in many ways. I attended services every Sunday because I was a "good Christian", or so I believed.

Then one Sunday, my pastor announced that a church near my home was holding a "Taize Service" that afternoon and recommended we should attend. I was interested and thought I would go until I got home from church. It was March, there was still snow on the ground, but it was melting; snow had turned to slush and puddles had become small ponds. By the time I walked from my car to my door my shoes and feet were soaked. So, I decided not to go out again and sat down to read the paper.

But, this was not to be; suddenly I realized I had put my shoes and coat back on and had walked the two blocks through the slush to the little church. I had no idea how or why I was there, but wet feet and all I decided that as long as I was there, I might as well stay.

If you have never attended a Taize service and an opportunity arises, I suggest you go. There is singing, readings of scripture, prayers, and periods of silent meditation. The songs are simple ones consisting of a few words repeated over and over. Then, midway through the service it happened!

The words we were singing were: "O Lord, hear my prayer. When I call, answer me". Suddenly I cried out loud: "Help me God, I need you so". Immediately my heart seemed to swell as if it would break and the sanctuary which was lit only by candles seemed to glow with a brilliant light. God had answered me and from that moment on my whole life had changed.

Yes, my life changed! I had always felt that I was a "Good Christian", but I quickly found out that was only partly right. In a blink of an eye God had entered my life and changed me forever. He had filled me with such joy and my heart with so much love that people said I glowed. My appreciation for the world around me deepened; I was no longer critical of others; rather I saw only good, not faults in them.

There were other changes also, such as a renewed desire to learn and the ability to write. However, the biggest and most important change was my relationship with God. Time spent in prayer had become quite sporadic, I rarely prayed at meal time and only occasionally at bed time. No longer was this to be! Now I began to really pray, to open my heart to God. At first, if I tried to crawl into bed or to fill my plate before I prayed, I would feel a nudge as if God was saying: "I'm waiting to hear from you" and I would respond in prayer immediately.

Day after day more and more times for prayer appeared. The first one was in the morning. No longer was ending the day with prayer enough; I needed to begin the day also. Some occasions could take considerable time while others might be just a few words. It didn't seem to matter just as long as I continued to pray.

I remember the first time I read Paul's words in 1Thessalonians 5:17: "Pray without ceasing". I wondered how one was to do this and still go about their daily lives, but it didn't take long for me to realize it could be done. Very shortly I found there were few moments that weren't times for prayer.

I had heard the expression "prayer life" before and soon came to realize this is what I now had. In time, opportunities for prayer appeared outside my normal daily life, but these I will cover later in the book.

This is approximately the point I was at in my previous book. I knew I could just mention the other occasions but in my heart I felt that would not be enough; there was far too much to say. So, I pulled out what I had written and thus this book was born. Prayer is far too important; is too much an integral part of a Christian's life not to be covered in totality. Thus we have a whole book on prayer. This is the "why" of this book!

PART I

WHAT IS PRAYER?

"Pray then in this way: Our Father
In Heaven, Hallowed be thy name."
Matthew 6:9

WHAT IS PRAYER? READING SCRIPTURE can be prayer. Have you ever recognized something in your life as you read of the cries of God's people held captive in Egypt, or read of the many trials of Job? As you read how God's powers brought happy endings for them, do you find yourself saying thankfully God was there for them and helped them: I pray he will do the same for me? This response is a prayer, a prayer for help.

150 of the Psalms are songs of prayer. I am sure most of you have memorized the 23rd Psalm as I have. It brought me tremendous comfort as I grieved the death of both of my parents. It brings me ease when I am sad, when I am troubled, or when I am just having a bad day. I say the words slowly and thoughtfully, often pausing as the words bring to mind a need; then I tell God my need, and I continue on. Each time I turn to this wonderful Psalm I know God is listening, I know he understands my needs; I know he will respond. He knows it is my heart speaking; he knows it is a prayer. When we are happy and want to share our joy with the Lord, or when we want to give thanks for his caring and for his gifts, what better place to turn to than to Psalm 100. For several years I lived in the foothills of southern California. Widowed

and raising 3 children on a small social security check, things often were very tight with only pennies left at the end of the month. I found that when I raised my eyes to the mountain tops and spoke the words of Psalm 121, God heard me and knew what I needed. Soon, almost miraculously, the needed help appeared.

Jesus also taught that our prayers must be real, honest, and sincere. We must not just speak empty words; we must express our thoughts and needs clearly. We must not stoop to bragging about ourselves; rather we must acknowledge ourselves as sinners. (Luke 18:10-13)

What is prayer? Music can be prayer. Mozart, Bach, Beethoven and many, many more great composers have written marvelous works, all dedicated to the glory of God. When I listen to "Ave Maria", I think of Mary, the woman God selected from all others to bear his Son. As I listen I cannot help but raise my eyes to heaven as I feel His love for us. Probably at the head of my list of great music has to be Handel's Messiah; a celebration of the life, death and resurrection of Christ.

Organ music before a service will prepare our minds and hearts for worship, the choir will present songs of praise, of worship, of love for God. In Psalm 95:2, David tells us: "Let us come into His presence with thanksgiving; let us make a joyful noise to him with songs of praise". This is what the choir does when they sing the anthems; this is what the congregation does when they lift their voices in hymns. I don't believe anyone can sing the hymn "Holy, Holy, Holy, Lord God Almighty: without feeling they are praying; nor can anyone sing the hymn; "I Need Thee Every Hour" without knowing they are praying for God to be in their lives. Whatever the means of presentation - a symphony orchestra, a small group of musicians, or a organ playing, the choir and/or the congregation singing, the result is the same. Their music is adoration and praise for the Lord. Their music is prayer.

What is prayer? When Jesus said: "Pray then in this way", He was giving us a prayer to be used; at the same time he was giving us a blueprint to use in our personal prayers. As I said in the beginning of this chapter, prayer is conversation with God. But when only one person speaks it is not a conversation, it is a lecture. Conversation requires us to both speak and then listen as the other speaks. Therefore, if prayer is conversation with God, we need to add another facet to Christ's blueprint; we also need to listen, listen for God's response. He won't speak to us personally as he did to Moses in Exodus 32:11-14, to Abraham in Genesis 18:23-33, or to Job in Job 40:6-24. His response may appear to be a still small voice in our minds, a stirring in our hearts to change something, or a sudden desire to do something. Whatever form it takes, God does respond.

Some people complain that they pray and pray, often for hours on end, but God doesn't answer their prayers. But, undoubtedly he would answer if they stopped talking long enough for him to get a few words in edge-wise. So, remember when you pray and you wish for an answer, shut your mouth, stop talking, and listen. In Psalm 46:10, we are told, "Be still and know that I am God". God hears you when you pray, he knows your needs and he will respond if you give him a chance. Listening for God to speak to us and to answer us should be a part of our prayers, for prayer is a cycle, we speak, God listens; God speaks, we listen.

What is prayer? Praise can be prayer; praise that acknowledges God's supremacy and his power. An example of this is the Doxology in which we state: "Praise God from whom all blessings flow, praise Him all creatures here below". Reading the Bible can also be prayer. Music can be prayer, but not much of what many of today's youth listen to. Some of this music is thoughtless, even nonsensical and sometimes promotes evil thoughts and deeds. The music I am speaking of is the music dedicated to God, the music which tells of His holiness, of His power, of His glory and, of His love for us and of our love for Him.

What is prayer? It is the raising of our minds and hearts to God. It can be more than the offering of our thoughts and acts to God, it can be an offering of ourselves, of who and what we are. We can do this with the help of the Holy Spirit as Paul says in Romans 8:26-27, "The Spirit helps us in our weakness; for we do not know how to pray as we ought, but that very Spirit intercedes with sighs too deep for words. And God, who searches the heart, knows what is in the mind of the Spirit, because the Spirit intercedes for the saints according to the will of God".

What is prayer? Everything mentioned in the previous paragraphs are kinds of prayer, but did you notice that they all have something in common? They all use words, words used to communicate with God. So, we have gone full circle and are back to the beginning of the chapter. What is prayer? Prayer is conversation with God.

PART II

WHY SHOULD WE PRAY?

"Do not worry about anything, but in everything by prayer and supplication with thanksgiving, let your request be made known to God."
Philippians 4:6

WHY SHOULD WE PRAY? WHY should we take time in our busy lives to speak to God? I believe a primary reason can be found in our basic need to communicate. Perhaps excepting those who are hermits, everyone feels this need at some time. But what do you do when you feel this need? Many of you will pick up the phone and call someone; others may write a letter. With today's technology, many will boot-up their computers and send out e-mails; others may text friends or family. Having done any or all of these has the need gone or is it still nagging our consciousness? Hopefully, through experience you have learned that this need will only be fully put to rest when you communicate with God. You need to pray.

Why should we pray? For years I shared my home in Maine with one of my daughters and her family. Then, one day after I retired from the Postal Service, I sold my home to her and moved to Wisconsin. There I lived alone but was not lonely because I communicated. For a while I communicated by phone with the daughter in Maine and with the daughter in California. But, as the saying goes: "I have more time than money:. The resulting phone bills were putting a big dent in my retirement check and both daughters were feeling the same thing. They kept asking why I didn't get a computer, but I kept making excuses. Finally they gave me one for my birthday. As I struggled to learn how to use it, I often prayed for patience, for help when nothing seemed to work right, and mostly for the wisdom to understand that frustrating machine. Finally, with help and guidance from friends and the Lord, I unraveled its mysteries and we could send emails or meet in a chat room. Time spent talking to my daughters, time spent with friends, time spent at church, all these helped fill my need to communicate. But, the nagging was often still there and was only satisfied when I communicated with the Lord in prayer.

Why should we pray? Wait a minute some of you say; "you are retired and have a lot of free time, but I have a family to care for and so I don't have the same luxury you have. My days are so full I seldom have a moment to think much less time to pray." Well I say, you may be busy, but I am sure the need to communicate is there and you find time to communicate with friends and family members even if just for a few moments. But, never forget that in Ephesians 2:19, Paul tells us "You are no longer strangers and aliens, but you are citizens with the saints and are also members of the household of God" So, if God is your heavenly Father and if you are his child, you should communicate with him too. You should pray.

Why should we pray? When we give a gift to someone and they just take it without even saying a simple thank you, our feelings are hurt and we may then decide never to give them another gift. Thankfully this is not God's way of doing things. He does have feelings and is hurt when we ignore the need to express our gratitude for the multitude of his gifts; but His love for us is so great that He continues to shower us with bounty. Look about you; the evidence of this is all about us and is there for all to see. So, unless you want to hurt God's feelings with a lack of appreciation and gratitude, you need to say thank you. You need to say it in prayer.

Why should we pray? Something wonderful has happened in your life; you get a promotion at work; one of your children gets all A's on their report card; your daughter or son receives a scholarship for college; maybe your family increases with the birth of a child or a grand-child. What do you do? Do you immediately send out e-mails, call friends and family, or do you drop in on a neighbor? You are so filled with joy you can't wait to share your happiness. But, aren't you forgetting someone; someone who used His awesome powers to put these events into motion? You need to shut down the computer, hang up the phone, say good-bye to the neighbor and tell God how happy you are. You need to pray!

Why should we pray? Everything that happens in our lives doesn't always bring joy and happiness. Far too often events bring about troubles, bring heartaches, and may even bring death and sorrow. You were hoping for a promotion and instead you got word that the company is going to down-size and your job is in jeopardy. What will you do if your job is lost you wonder, since times are tough and few jobs are available. Your son falls off his bicycle and breaks his arm. Now he just sits around crying. He is broken-hearted because he cannot pitch in the championship game with a cast on his arm. Your daughter will never get to use her scholarship; anxious to share the good news with her best friend, she didn't look before she pulled into the intersection and didn't see the truck coming. She was killed in the resulting accident.

What do you do when bad things happen? Do you sit for hours with tears flowing, crying out: "Why me, oh why is this happening to me?" Do you throw up your hands and say: "what's the use, no matter how hard I try nothing ever seems to go right?" Do you refuse to face your troubles or your loss, retreating into yourself and become a virtual zombie? Or.......do you dry your tears, straighten your shoulders, and set about bringing some sense and order back into your life? If so, this is the perfect time to open your heart and talk to God. This is the time to pray!

Why should we pray? We are told that our prayers should begin with praise for the Lord, for his omnipotence, and for his love. This should be followed by confession of our sins. When that first bite was taken of that apple in the Garden, sin entered the world and from that moment to today, all God's children are sinners. God's promise of forgiveness was given when his Son was crucified for our sins. However, although God always keeps his promises, forgiveness does not come automatically. He does not want us to have hearts heavy and dark because of the sins they hold. In Psalm 51:3, David says: "I know my transgressions and my sin is always before me". Here David is admitting that he has sinned, is admitting it openly and honestly. This is what God wants; he wants us to empty our hearts of sins as we honestly and humbly acknowledge them. He wants us to pray!

No matter how hard we try, we all sin. Day after day, in big ways or in small ways, we break one or more of God's Commandments. You should never feel they were set aside when Jesus said the greatest ones are: "Love the Lord with all your heart, all you soul and all your mind" and "Love your neighbor as yourself". (Matthew 22:37, 39) If you read on to verse 40, He says: "On these two commandments hang all the law". Furthermore, in Matthew 5:17, he tells us: "Do not think that I have come to abolish the law or the prophets; I have come not to abolish but to fulfill".

As Christians we are a people chosen by God; we have been called for a purpose known only to God. We have been created to worship him and part of worship is obedience to his will. God knows his people's weaknesses. He knows they will often give in to temptation; knows they will act rashly and in haste without considering the consequences. He knows they will continue to ignore his wishes unless they become etched in stone. So, his mighty fingers began their work and the Commandments were given to Moses.

People today sin just as much if not more than people did back then, and therefore, anyone who believes that the Ten Commandments no longer have a place in our lives are very, very wrong. God says they do when in Exodus 20:6 He says He will show steadfast love to the thousandth generation of those who keep his Commandments. In fact, they have to have a place if we are to live the life God wishes us to. If you still doubt, they do have a place today, please read on.

1 - Thou shall have to other gods before me.

Do I hear some of you protesting that you never break this commandment? You may claims that you worship only God, not idols. But are you sure? True, when you attend church services you worship God, and only God. But, how about once you walk out the door of the church? What about the rest of the week? Unfortunately, far too many of us focus on achieving fame and fortune; and the pursuit of money and/or material goods take over our lives. Then, where is God? He has been relegated to a corner of our consciousness, only to be brought forth the next Sunday when we go to church. Other pursuits have taken his place in our lives.

II - You shall not make wrongful use
      of the name of the Lord.

You say you never curse or swear so you do not break this commandment. Again I say, are you sure? Remember, God's name was so revered that ancient peoples were forbidden to even speak it. When Moses asked God what name to call him, he was told: "I am who I am". Even Moses, chosen by God to lead his people out of slavery, was not to speak His name. It was Christ who revealed that God is a God of love, and now, although we can speak his name we must treat it with reverence. Of course we must not curse, but we must also not use it casually. How often, in a moment of surprise, of exasperation, or of disgust, have you said: "Oh God, now what?" Or maybe: "Oh lord, not again?". This too is wrong. The ability to speak God's name is a gift, a gift to be used in worship. To use it in thoughtless, casual conversation is not acceptable; it is as much a sin as cursing.

III - Observe the Sabbath Day and keep it Holy.

Each Sunday most pastors begin the service by saying: "This is the day the Lord has made, let us rejoice and be glad in it". This is more than a statement of fact; it is more than a call to worship; it is a call to fulfill God's commandment,

When God created the world's inhabitants, it was not His intention that they should work. But a single bite of the forbidden fruit changed his plan and so mankind was sent out to toil the rest of their lives. But, God in His omnipotence knew that mankind would need a day of rest, just as God had. The hour or so we spend in worship is good; it is how we spend the remaining 23 hours that often is wrong. Unfortunately, today's society is at odds with God's commandment. Schools schedule sports and other events on Sundays. Major league sports always have Sunday afternoon and evening games and far too many people will even skip attending worship so they can be in the stadium in time for the kick-off or the first pitch. Most stores are open, forcing employees to work, and creating the temptation to spend a good part of the day shopping. Many spend the day doing chores and odd jobs they have put off doing all week long. Then there are the workaholics who bring work home and spend the day doing the same things they do all week long on the job.

So, what are we to do? Are we to do nothing on the Sabbath, not even cook meals as the ancient Israelites were told? Jesus told us it was all right to do things on the

Sabbath as long as they are done for good. In today's world there are some who need to work on Sunday. Policemen and firemen are needed for emergencies and for our safety. Hospitals cannot send the patients home and then close the doors for the day, so doctors and nurses must be on duty. But, stores do not need to be open on Sunday. There are six other days in the week when people can shop. When we shop on Sunday we are doubly wrong; not only are we not resting, neither are those who are waiting on us. As for the workaholic, why does he feel the need to work on Sunday? Is the job too much to handle in a normal work week? Or is he doing extra work while striving for a raise or promotion? Whatever the reasons, they should be examined closely and decide is they really are more important the obeying God's commandment.

When God finished creating the world and its inhabitants, he said: "It is good:" and then he rested. This is what he wishes for his people; six days of labor and then a day of rest. When we keep the Sabbath holy, a day for worship; when we keep it as a day of rest, we are obeying the Lord. The Sabbath is a time for re-creation not recreation. It is a time to remember that we are all children of God, created to worship him. It is a time to re-create ourselves in the image of Christ, a time to make Sunday truly "The Lord's Day".

IV - Honor your father and your mother

We were created to need others and that is a foundation of the Christian life. Fulfillment of this need begins at the moment of conception, continues as the mother nurtures the unborn infant is her womb, and from birth on, both parents work to provide for the infant's every need. But, parents should do more than care for their child's needs. They should be examples of living according to God's will. They should be teachers, telling the child about God and what he wishes for their lives. Most of all they should teach them of God's love by loving them as God does.

It is a fact that not all parents are good parents; some do not nurture and care for their children, and therefore are not deserving of the honor given them by God. However, when a child is baptized, the whole church accepts responsibility for them and for their faith. Thus, they can be rescued from a non-nurturing family and be adopted into a new family, the church.

When God said: "Be fruitful and multiply", he created parenthood. When he did so, he made parents his representatives on earth. It is they who are to nurture and care for God's children. It is a high vocation through which God continues creation and thus is worthy of honor.

V - You shall not kill

God says we should not kill.........period. He does not say unless, or if, or because; his statement is unconditional. He will not accept any reason or excuse. The dictionary defines the word kill as an unlawful taking of another's life. Unfortunately this is the loophole which governments use. They pass laws which in their eyes make it legal.

Governments send young people off to war, justifying it by saying it is to defend the country or to help another country. Sometimes they do not even try to justify it; they do it to take another country's land or possessions. They may claim it is "the right thing to do", but they are wrong. There is no such thing as a righteous war.

Governments pass laws allowing the execution of some who are convicted of heinous crimes. When their right to do this is questioned, they often will quote Exodus 21:23 by saying: 'An eye for an eye". But remember, God of the Old Testament was often a God of wrath and vengeance, a God to be feared. Jesus changed this when he taught us that God is a God of love and not to be feared. In Matthew 5:38-39, he says that exacting an eye for an eye is wrong; rather we are to turn the other cheek. In Matthew 5:43-44, he tells us we should not hate our enemies, we should love them and pray for them. If we obey Christ, how can we execute someone, someone which He tells us we should love.

I wonder what God's reaction was when the courts declared that abortion was legal. He must have said: "How dare you......I created what you wish to destroy....you don't have the right". God had already given his people the necessary means for accomplishment when he told them to be fruitful and multiply, but when they multiply is not up to them. This decision is God's alone and when he feels the time is right, it is his mighty powers that cause the two cells to unite. People may feel this burgeoning being is theirs to do with as they please, but they are very wrong. It is not theirs, it is God's. It is a gift given to them in trust that they will tend to its every need. When they decide to end its life before it is born, they are breaking this trust with God. They are sinning.

From the day that Cain slew Abel to the present day, people have disobeyed God's commandment and have killed others. Criminals kill during the commission of a crime; there are gang wars and drive-by shootings; we have road rage, suicides, and killings done in moments of anger or distress. Governments tell us it is ok to kill as long as we do it within the boundaries of their laws. Whatever the cause, the reason, or the supposed justification, to kill another is wrong. When someone takes the life of another, they are taking the place of God. They are usurping his powers, because all life belongs to Him and only He has the right to end it.

VI - You shall not commit adultery.

During the marriage ceremony both the bride and groom vow to love and honor each other, forsaking all others. This promise is given not only to each other, it is also given to God. With the final words: "I now pronounce you man and wife", the two become one, become a unit called family. God was present; he listened to the exchange of vows. He knew this newly created family now had the right to be fruitful and multiply and he knew it should only be with each other. It is those three words, "forsaking all others" that are the keystone of their marriage.

Jesus knew the importance of this commandment. He not only speaks of it, he expands its perimeters. In Matthew 5:28, he says: "Everyone who looks at a woman with lust has already committed adultery in his heart". I am sure if he was present today and was confronted by the endless parade of nudity and near-nudity, he would expand even further and say that even to look and admire and think of what one would like to do is also adultery.

Jesus did not stop with one addition, he also included divorce. In Matthew 19:5-6, he says that man shall leave his father and mother and be joined to his wife, becoming one flesh and what God has joined no one may separate. In verse 9, he says whoever divorces and remarries commits adultery.

Paul takes this Commandment even further when in Corinthians 6, he warns against fornication, against sex outside of the sanctity of marriage. He says we become one with the body of Christ when we are baptized and thus, when we have sex with someone without marriage, we are sinning; we are committing adultery against Christ.

Today many people treat sex far too casually. They even give the act names like scoring, hitting, hooking up, or reach third base. Those who abstain are often looked at as being less than a normal person, perhaps even looked at as being gay. Our lives have become sex--filled; movies, TV, and ads have made it a commodity to be desired. This is not God's wish! When he created man differently he did it so they could be fruitful, have children, and raise them to His glory. This is his plan, to do anything else is a sin.

VII - You shall not steal.

Of course we should not steal. Everything we have is a gift, given to us by God and no one has the right to take another's gift and claim it as their own. To do this is to say that God made a mistake and gave it to the wrong person. But, God does not make mistakes and to say he does so is a sin in its self.

There are more facets to stealing other than taking another's possessions. When we tell a lie about someone, this can bring about shame and to cause shame is stealing. Yes, it is stealing because we have taken away a part of their self-respect, of their reputation, perhaps even of their confidence.

When we refuse to give someone their due, we are stealing. Suppose a workman comes to your home and does some repairs or fixes something that is broken. When he is finished, you refuse to pay him. You now have stolen what is rightly his as payment for his labors.

You are in the grocery store; your wallet is quite full as are your cupboards, fridge and freezer. As you put your few items in the little basket, you recall hearing that the local food pantry is badly in need of food. What do you do? Do you go back, get a big cart, fill it, pay for it and take the items to the food pantry? Or, do you make excuses like: "I don't have time today, maybe next week", or "the pantry is way over on the other side of town and I am already running late". Hopefully you got the cart and filled it because to not do it is stealing, stealing food from the hungry when you have the means to provide it.

Perhaps one winter day your doorbell rings. When you open the door you see a man standing there. Through chattering teeth he offers to shovel the snow off your sidewalk. He is shivering badly and you realize he is wearing only shorts and a tee shirt. What do you do? Do you invite him inside to warm up and then give him one of the many coats hanging in the closet? Or, do you just shut the door and leave him standing out in the cold? If this is what you do, you are stealing also. You are stealing the warmth and comfort he so badly needed.

Why have I placed so much emphasis on not helping the needy? In the first place, to help the needy is what Jesus told us we must do. His words in Matthew 25:40: "Just as you did it to one of the least of whom are members of my family, you did it to me." Leave no doubt, we must never forget that all we have is not ours, it is God's. It was given to us as a gift in trust that we will not clutch it to ourselves, but, will use it to help others in their need. To not do so is to steal.

VIII - You shall not bear false witness
against your neighbor

Have you ever been called to be a witness in court? If so, what was the first thing you were required to do? I am sure you raised your right hand and promised to the truth, the whole truth, and nothing but the truth. To lie after making this promise can cause great harm. A lie told to help the accused runs the risk of setting a guilty person free, possibly to commit another crime. At the same time you are saying that the accusers lied. A lie told to help the accusers may cause an innocent person to be incarcerated or possibly even to be executed.

I am not sure, but I believe that due to the workings of a misguided few you no longer place your hand on a Bible while taking the oath. Whether you do or not, remember that God is omnipresent and He heard you. Therefore, if you break your promise and lie to the court, you are also lying to God. You have broken his Commandment.

The courtroom is not the only place where people can bear false witness. People love to gossip and seldom bother to ascertain the truth before they repeat what they heard. What they heard may have been passed on so many times that there is no longer much resemblance to what was originally said and it has become a lie. I remember playing a game we called "telephone". A group would sit in a circle, a sentence or two would be whispered in the ear of the first player and then was passed on by a whisper in the ear of each in turn. When the final person would repeat out loud what they heard or thought they heard, there was seldom little if any left of what was first said. This is a prime example of the danger of repeating gossip; it may now be a complete lie, in fact may have been so from the beginning.

We all tend to lie at times. We tell "little white lies" for a variety of reasons. At times we tell them for our own benefit, maybe to make ourselves look good, maybe to cover up another lie, or possibly to white-wash something we have done. We may tell them to keep from hurting someone's feelings. We often tell these "little lies" with the attitude of "who cares, no one got hurt". Wrong, God got hurt when we disobeyed his Commandment.

When God created us, he gave each of us a tongue. In the book of James, the author devotes Chapter three to the need to tame the tongue. Here he says the tongue is a fire and can be like a flame that sets a great forest on fire. I have seen these great fires and I know it takes no more than a discarded cigarette or a spark from a carelessly built campfire to start one. I also know it is very difficult to put it out once it is started. I have seen the damage these fires do, so I can understand why James has said we need to tame our tongues. Like the spark that starts the forest fire, once the tongue releases the words of a lie they cannot be taken back. They are out there and the damage they can cause begins.

It doesn't matter what reason or excuse you use when you tell a lie; it doesn't matter if it is a little white one or a whopper; the truth is that a lie is a lie, is a lie, is a lie. And to lie is a sin.

IX and X - You shall not covet.

The final two Commandments both tell us it is a sin to want the possessions of others. I feel it would only invite repetition to look at them separately and therefore will treat them as one.

When God gave his Commandments to Moses many, many years ago, people's lives were different from most of ours today. I often wonder if God has ever considered updating them to better fit today's society. If he were to do so, I am sure he would immediately change the word wife to either mate or to spouse because in most parts of today's world women are no longer considered to be a subservient people; women's lib changed that. However, along with equal rights come equal obligations and an equal admonition not to covet. Webster defines the word covet as the wish to have, to want, to desire. I am not sure why these definitions were placed in this particular order, but I find it very indicative of the way the human mind often works. We may begin by just admiring a possession of someone; soon that admiration turns to the wish to have; the wish quickly turns to want and ultimately wants turns to desire. But desire does not stand alone; it can carry the evils of envy, greed, and even lust. It is at this point that people say: "I don't care what it takes, I will have it". It is at this point we strike a blow to the loving heart of God. It is at this point we sin.

When God wrote his Commandments, he set them in a definite order. The first four, from worshiping Him and only Him, to not miss-using his name, to keeping the Sabbath holy and to honoring our parents leave no doubt that these are his desires. These are what he commands us to do. The other six tell us what we must not do. Here again I wonder if God were to re-write the Commandments would he move the seventh one to be the fifth? Why do I say this? I say it because I have already shown that each of the final six involve stealing in one form or another.

I do not feel the last two were placed at the end because God felt they were less important. I feel they are where they are because they sum up all the "You shall not's" and when we break these two we can also break some or all of the others at the same time.

I have used a lot of words to show that the Ten Commandments do still matter in our lives today. If any of you still feel differently I suggest that you should go back and read this whole section again.........because you are still wrong. For those who felt they were looking in a mirror and seeing yourself as you read, now is the time. Now is the time to talk to God. Now is the time to tell him all you found hidden in the dark recesses of your heart? Now is the time to ask his forgiveness. Now is the time for prayer.

WHY DON'T WE PRAY?

WHY DON'T WE PRAY? IN our busy lives why don't we take the time to pray? Why should we use our precious moments to speak to God when we have been told that He knows what we would say even before we speak?

I'm too busy to pray is the number one excuse used, but a prayer need not be prolonged. It does not even need to be out loud since God knows our thoughts and will hear them. While cooking a meal, doing household chores, during a coffee break or lunch, or even while driving your car can be times available to speak with God. Our time on earth is ours to use as we wish, a gift from the loving heart of God. Our days, our weeks, our years are given to us freely with no strings attached. If we were to ask God, I am sure he would tell us to use this time wisely and not waste it in idle preoccupation. When you get up in the morning, don't waste time thinking of all that you have to do, or worrying about potential problems that may never occur. Instead, use these moments for prayer. Doing this can ease your mind, can lighten your heart, and then you will be able to face the day with joy. Spending time in prayer is always a wise use of time. I have no time to pray is a poor excuse for not praying!

Why don't we pray? Perhaps we feel too independent. From early childhood we are taught to be self-reliant. Many books have been written teaching us to "do it ourselves". These books are fine for home repairs or fixing faulty plumbing, but they are no help with physical or emotional troubles. Today's culture tells us we can solve our problems on our own, often telling us we need to just take a pill or two and our troubles will go away. But, pills do not cure the problem; they merely give us a false sense of security and well-being. When we feel our lives are in turmoil and our world is falling apart, we may come to the point where we feel we can no longer cope. In the Bible in 1 John 5:14-15, we are told: "This is the boldness we have in Him, that if we ask anything according to his will, he hears us. And if we know that he hears us in whatever we ask, we know that we have obtained the requests made of him". We need to take our troubles to God, need to do it in prayer and ask for his help. I don't need help, I can do it myself is a poor excuse for not praying!

Why don't we pray? Maybe we feel intimidated, feel we just won't do it right. We have all heard long, eloquent prayers and may have come away with the feeling the prayers is beyond our abilities. These prayers are wonderful, but so are simple prayers. Think of prayer as being like communicating with a loved one far away. A long detailed letter would be great, but then again even a postcard will bring joy to the heart of the one receiving it, just as even a simple brief prayer will bring joy to God. There is no right or wrong time to pray. Prayer is merely conversation and you can talk to your Heavenly Father just as easily and simply as you would to your earthly one. Intimidation or fear are both poor excuses for not praying!

In Matthew 8:23-26, we are told that Jesus and his disciples got in a boat. He must have been tired because he didn't pick up oars and help row across the sea. He fell asleep! Suddenly the wind rose and tossed the boat about; the waves grew to great heights and water was filling the boat. The disciples were afraid; they knew they were in trouble so they woke Jesus crying: "We are perishing". But Jesus wasn't afraid, he didn't panic; he just spoke to the wind and the sea. We aren't told exactly what he said, but if he had used language common today, he probably would have said something like: "Enough already! Stop this right now!" Whatever words he said, they worked and the wind and sea were calmed.

In Matthew 14:23-24, we are told that the disciples were again crossing the sea in a boat. But this time Jesus was not with them, he had gone up the mountain to pray. Now, some of the disciples were seasoned fishermen. They had spent their lives on this sea and when the wind suddenly changed direction and now blew in their faces, they knew there would be hard work ahead,. They knew they could merely turn the boat around and, with the wind at their backs, easily make it back to the shore. But, they also knew they had to go forward... because this is what Jesus told them to do. Where was Jesus? He was still on the mountain. He had to have felt the wind switch direction and increase in strength. He had to know what that would mean for the men in the boat. He knew he could help them. But he had come up on the mountain to pray so he stayed where he was. In the meantime, the disciples were struggling. At first they were sure they would be all right; they had faced such winds before. However, this time the harder they rowed, the harder the wind blew. Their arms became tired and each stroke of the oars was agony. I can only imagine what had to be going through their minds as they fought the tempest. "Where is Jesus? Why did he send us out here with a storm brewing? We saw him calm the winds before, so why isn't he here now to help us?"

The writers of the Gospels must have realized the importance of this story, because it can be found in several of them. In fact, in Mark 6:52, Mark says that their hearts had been hardened. Is he suggesting that perhaps the disciples' distress could have been caused by more that the storm? Does he feel they could have been upset with Jesus; upset because their feelings had been hurt? As they struggled to make head-way against the wind, could they have been grumbling to each other or maybe just thinking: "How can He treat us like he has today? We have followed him faithfully and have done all he asked us to do. He sent us out to preach and heal. When we returned and told him all we had done, did he prepare a feast to celebrate our accomplishments? No way, he sent us on our way without so much as a crust of bread. We were there all day while he preached to the crowds and healed their sick. Then when it was getting late we told him the people had to be hungry; told him we didn't have enough money to buy food for so many, told him he should send them home. Did he listen to us? No, he didn't, he told us to feed them and when we said it couldn't be done, he proceeded to feed that multitude with just five loaves and two fish. We thought we had given him good advice, but he showed us how little our advice meant. Then what did he do? Although, with signs of bad weather approaching, he ordered us into the boat and told us to go to the other side, and He didn't even come with us; he went off by himself. We don't deserve to be treated this way".

Of course these words of the disciples won't be found in the Bible. They are mine. Mark merely said their hearts had hardened. But I know a hardened heart is a darkened heart; I know the joy of life will be missing and so will be any happy thoughts. I know that thoughts like those I attributed to the disciples can easily take over. The disciples felt unappreciated; they may have even felt deserted by Jesus. After all, he was safe and sound on land while they were in the midst of a battle, a battle the wind was winning. Every bit of forward progress they managed to achieve was quickly erased as the wind and waves pushed them backwards. They had seen storms like this before. They had seen broken boats washed up on the shore after such a storm. They knew there was a good chance they would all die. They had to be crying out "Where are you, Jesus? You can still the storm as you did before. You can save us. We cannot do it ourselves". They knew Jesus could help, but they apparently never thought to ask God for help, never stopped grumbling long enough to pray. The disciples had faced the storms, unhappy and grumbling, but confident they could handle it. However they soon found that knowledge of the sea and years of experience on it were not enough. The storm was defeating them and they knew they needed help.

At times we too can all face storms. I am not speaking of thunderstorms, of tornadoes, or even of hurricanes. I mean a storm that enters your life and can turn it up-side down. I mean a storm that enters your life unexpected and turns what had been peace into chaos. When you encounter such a storm in your life, what do you do? Some of you will probably just try to handle it yourself, probably only making matters worse. What do you do then? Others may muddle along, not really sure what you are doing or how to handle it. Then, totally frustrated, you may turn to a friend or family member. They may say: "Been there, done that", and proceed to tell you how they handled their storm. But, when you try to follow their advice, it doesn't work and things only got worse. What do you do then? Why do you not pray?

What storms have you encountered? Perhaps one appeared when the doctor called and said, "I'm afraid I have bad news"; maybe one started with a letter from the IRS stating that they found an error and you now owe many dollars, a letter that came only 2 days after you bought new furniture and nearly wiped out your bank account. Could one appear when someone from the school office calls and tells you that your son did not arrive that day? They go on to say one of the classmates says they saw him talking to a man in a blue car.

What do you do when a storm disrupts your life? Do you say: "I can handle it", and set out to ride it out on your own? If so, you should consider the following hypothetical case to see how successful or unsuccessful to do so can be.

You have invited your boss and his wife over for dinner; you want to make a good impression so you look around the house to make sure everything is ready. All looks great and the aromas from the kitchen set your taste buds to water, so you decide to sit and relax for a few minutes. But you are barely seated when you hear a scream and an anguished cry, "Honey, come here… quickly". You enter the kitchen to find the cold water running and your wife holding the handle to the faucet in her hand. "What happened?" You ask. She responds saying, "I don't know, it just came off in my hand". "No problem" you say as you grab a screwdriver. But, you don't hold the screw right and the threads strip. Now it won't tighten. "No problem" you say, it will work without a screw. However, you turn the handle the wrong way and now the water pours out. "No problem" you say, I'll just use the shut-off under the sink. But the shut-off refuses to turn. "No problem" you say again as you find a wrench which turns out is too small. "No problem", you say as you look behind the shut-off. The little wrench will fit here and you begin to turn only to find it is not part of the shut-off, it is not a handle, it is a pipe and suddenly it comes apart. Now the water isn't pouring into the sink, it is pouring out onto the floor. Within minutes the kitchen floor is flooded, the dining room carpet is wet, and the water is nearing the living room. You stand helplessly asking yourself "Oh why didn't I call the plumber?" Your wife is yelling: "Look at the mess you made". She is right. You did make a mess and you don't know it yet, but the mess is about to get worse. The water is still pouring out, you are groaning, your wife is crying and then suddenly you hear bells ringing. It is the doorbell, and your company has arrived. What a perfect time for prayer before you open the door.

Of course I made up this story, but it could have happened. In fact similar storms probably already have happened to someone, somewhere, sometime. What did they do? Did they try to do it themselves and as a result cause what had been just a gentle springtime rain to escalate into a destructive tornado? Or, did they try for a bit, find they couldn't handle it, and then looked for help?

If you are wondering why I have used so much space talking about storms when this is a book about prayer, you have missed my point completely. I told these stories because I felt they carried a lesson; told these stories to illustrate a message I was trying to convey. "What message?" you say! Well, here is the message in a much shorter form.

We all have storms in our lives; unexpected events, even fear or the loss of a loved one can bring one about. Whatever the cause, the result is the same; they all disrupt our lives and often bring about turmoil. What can we do? We can try to calm the storm ourselves; or we can look for help and what better place to look than to God. The purpose of prayer is not to influence God to grant favors, but to remind you that you are connected to God. After all, prayer is the recognition that Christ is knocking at the door to our heart and it is opening the door and saying: "come in".

God loves us and he loves to help us. But, he doesn't want us to sit idly and wait for him to solve all our problems, to calm our storms. He will give us the strength and confidence to us our talents so we can start to work. He wants us to use whatever talents he gave us, wants us to do our part, then he will do the rest. God is waiting patiently to help us, but he will only help when we ask, when we ask in prayer. Whatever the size or form of the storm; whether we can handle and calm the storm ourselves or not; we need God. We need to pray! This is my message.

PART III

WHEN SHOULD WE PRAY?

"Rejoice always, pray without ceasing, give thanks in all circumstances, for this is the will of God in Christ Jesus for you."
I Thessalonians 5: 16-18

CHAPTER I

WHEN SHOULD WE PRAY?

WHEN SHOULD WE PRAY? I could end this part of my book quickly by merely saying "always". In Philippians 4:6, Paul tells us: "Do not worry about anything, but in everything by prayer and supplication with thanksgiving let your requests be made known unto God". In Colossians 4:2 he says: "Devote yourselves to prayer, keeping alert in it with thanksgiving". There are monks who obey these commands; they devote their every waking moment to prayer. But, we are not monks, shut away from the outside world in a monastery; we are ordinary people with ordinary busy lives.

When should we pray? When Paul said we should devote our lives to prayer, I do not believe he was telling us to live as monks do. He didn't! If he had spent his life on his knees in prayer, when would he have had time to write all his letters? When could he have traveled afar to establish and then visit all those burgeoning churches? As we read his letters the fact that he did pray and did pray often is apparent. Over and over we find the words "pray and prayer" as he writes: "In my prayers I ask", "I pray that", or "I pray for". The love for the Lord and the need to pray were always in his heart and mind, and whenever he felt the need, he knew it was the time for prayer.

When should we pray? Jesus knew when it was time! He prayed when he raised Lazarus from the dead; praying then so the people would believe, believe he was sent by God (John 11:41-42). He blessed the loaves and fish when He fed the multitude (Matthew 14:19). Then, after he dismissed the crowd, he went alone up the mountain to pray. He prayed in Gethsemane. He prayed as he was dying on the cross, asking not for an end to his agony, but rather, for forgiveness for those who has nailed him to the cross. I am sure there were many more times during his time on earth that Jesus felt the need to talk to his Father. He knew when it was time to pray, so he prayed.

When should we pray? I no longer wonder when I should pray, wonder if it is the right time or place; I just pray. I begin my day with scripture, then the Lord's Prayer. Then I open my heart and release any worries, troubles, fears, or joys. God is there with me, He listens, and when I finish I am ready to face the day with a light heart. What better way to start the day.

God expects us to pray because it can stir him into action. He listens, he hears, and if needed he acts on our behalf. Do not hesitate to cry out to God and ask anything. We are told in Hebrews 4:16: "Come boldly unto the throne of grace, that you may obtain mercy and find grace in time of need".

As I take daily walks, I do not walk alone. God is with me and I continuously talk to him as I walk. The glory of a sunrise, a much needed rain, the beauty of nature, a lovely flower bed, no matter what my eyes behold, I cannot help but express my gratitude for his love and for the bounty with which he fills the earth. I don't make a mental note to thank him the next morning in my prayers, I do it right away. That is the right time to pray.

God has given me the wonderful gift of the ability to write. My first book has been published and I am now working on this new one. As I write, I occasionally meet an impasse; I know what I want to say but the right words just won't come. I have found that a simple prayer: "Help me please Lord, help me to find the words I need" will bring instant assistance and the words will again flow. I also spend many hours doing handcrafts; I make most of my gifts for friends and family as well as make many items for church craft sales, but my greatest love is doing counted cross-stitch. I have made a reproduction of the Last Supper. The pattern came with over 50 different colors of threads and as I worked I needed to count and watch each stitch. As I began working each time, I asked the Lord to guide my hand so I would get it correct and not have to take any stitches out one by one. When I finished each figure and saw it was correct I then thanked God for his help. Hour after hour, day after day, no matter what I am doing, I communicate with the Lord. He listens, he cares, and when needed, he answers. I am at peace, but only as long as I continue to pray.

When should we pray? Some of you may be stay-at-home parents, others may be part of a two-job family. In either case, your days are similar, especially if you have children. The start of the day can be hectic until the kids are fed, dressed, and off to school or wherever. For you stay-at-home parents, why not try something different;

instead of mentally thinking about all you need to do today, pause and take a deep breath. Then take a few moments to talk to God. You can continue to talk to Him as you work. The spilled juice you need to clean up, the never-ending piles of laundry, the house that always seems to need cleaning or straightening, the food you need to go purchase and later prepare; all of these are gifts from God. When you receive a gift from someone, you thank them. So, shouldn't you do the same for God? Paul sums things up this way. He says it is God's will for us to be thankful in all circumstances. When things seem to go against us, God expects us to be grateful that his hand holds us and helps us endure. This is a good time to say thank you in prayer. It can be equally difficult to the thankful when things are going well. Sound strange? After all, when things go well, we have even more to be thankful for. But the nature of human beings is to overlook the volume of good gifts God gives us every day. So, why not talk to him as you go about your daily chores and offer your thanks for his bounty? He will listen; he will even hear you over the noisy clothes washer or the vacuum cleaner.

When should we pray? For those who have jobs to go to daily, don't turn on the radio or slip in a CD as you drive to work; you could use this time to pray. But, make sure the radio is turned off, not just down, or you could become distracted. If you take a bus or use other means of public transportation, you too can use travel time to pray. It needn't be out loud or people could think you are strange. Say the words silently in your mind and God will hear them since he knows your every thought. Your job, the clothes you wear, the home you have, even the foods you eat; all these are gifts, are parts of God's bounty. Since everything you have is given to you by God in his grace, why not tell him how thankful you are? In Ephesians 5:15-16, Paul tells us: "Be careful how you live...making the most of every opportunity". Don't put it off, do it now. Now is the time to pray! When should we pray? Is there a right time as well as a wrong time? I do not think there is ever a wrong time, what do you think?

What would you do if you are cooking dinner and a friend calls saying they have something wonderful to tell you? Do you take the chance that the dinner will burn and listen? Or do you say "I can't talk now but I'll call you soon and you can tell me then". You were too busy to listen; would God ever be? When something wonderful happens in your life and you want to share your joy with the Lord in prayer, would he say: "Not now, I'll let you know when I have time to listen?" Of course not, He is never too busy to hear from us.

What would you do if you are watching your favorite TV show and it is at a crucial point when one of your children comes running crying out that they need your help with their homework. Do you turn off the TV and go see if you can help? Or do you say "You'll have to wait until this program is finished"? You're too busy to give help when asked; would God be? He loves to help us; we need only to ask. He would never say: "I'm doing something else right now, but I'll see what I can do for you later". He waits patiently to hear us say the words: "I need help". Then his great power will go to help us. He is never too busy when we ask for help!

Your best friend's loved one has passed away and you hear that she isn't coping well with her grief. You remember the comfort she brought you when your mother passed away and you know you should go to her. What do you do? Do you hop in your car and go immediately to offer solace? Or do you put it off saying: "I cannot go today, I have a important meeting; I cannot go tomorrow as I have a dentist appointment; maybe the next day or two I can make it". You were too busy to give comfort and to ease the grief of someone you cared for; would God be? Could He ever say to a grieving person: "I'm sorry but today is the harp orchestra's concert and I'm the conductor so I have to be there; tomorrow I have scheduled a conference with my Son and the Prophets to go over my plans for the future; but, you should be okay for a day or two and I will try to make time for you as soon as I can". God would never turn his back on someone needing comfort; his arms are always wide open waiting to hold us and ease our pain.

When should we pray? Could there ever be a wrong time? Could God ever be too to listen to our prayer? Could he ever be too busy to help us when we ask? Could he ever make excuses and expect us to bear our troubles ourselves, bear our grief, until he gets around to helping? Of course not! He is never too busy to listen to our prayers. If you feel there is a wrong time, perhaps it is because you do not trust his promise to listen; perhaps it is because you have prayed and felt you have not gotten the response you expected; or perhaps you feel that you are unworthy.

It is not always easy to trust someone, but there is one we can trust......always. God does not lie, not that he will not, but that he cannot. So, when he says we can trust him, we can believe his words. There can be many reasons why a prayer is not answered. Perhaps the prayer was for the wrong thing or reason. There are some requests which God will not answer, especially for one that will bring about self-aggrandizement. Then again, maybe the prayer was answered and you didn't realize it. God does not always give an immediate response; He does things in his own time according to his own plans. Perhaps your request could only be answered in steps and you got tired of waiting before the steps were completed and so didn't recognize the response. As for being unworthy, there is no one so given to sin and evil that God won't forgive them. His Son didn't die for the sins only of those God felt worthy of forgiveness, He died for the sins of all God's peoples. Remember, Christ even forgave the thief hanging on the next cross and promised him a place in heaven. How can you feel you are unworthy? God loves you, He will listen, and He will answer. You need only to pray!

When should we pray? Perhaps you feel it is not the right time because you are so upset you can't seem to stop crying. You are so upset you can barely think or speak coherently. This is the time you need most to pray. I had such a time when I returned to my home after watching the film "The Passion of Christ". To say that I was upset would be putting it mildly. I could not seem to stop crying my clothes were soaked with tears and I could barely remain standing. Suddenly I began to scream, not as a person normally screams, I was screaming at God. Over and over I yelled out the words: "How could you? How could a loving father force his son to suffer so? Why, oh why did you do that?" On and on I continued until my throat was so raw I could no longer scream. I fell to the ground and must have dozed off for a bit. When I woke up I realized what I had done and I was horrified. How did I dare to yell at the Lord? In my heart I knew it was true, I had done it, but it was difficult for me to accept. If I closed my eyes, the scenes of the whippings and the crucifixion were etched on my eyelids. I was ashamed at what I had done, but one thing I did know was that no matter what I did, God loved me. So, I hoped he understood why I did it. So, I did what I knew I had to do… I prayed, asking His forgiveness. His answer came quickly as I got the desire to write, write what was still burning in my heart. This is what I wrote……….

"Did He Need to Suffer and Die?

Was the suffering and death of Christ really necessary? Couldn't He just have come to earth, fulfilled his ministry, and then merely returned home to the Father? God, in his wisdom, knew this would not be enough.

When Adam and Eve disobeyed him, God didn't just scold them, He banished then from the Garden forever. As the people multiplied, so did their wickedness. In Genesis 6:6-7, we are told that God was so grieved that he decided to destroy all living things he had created. He saved only Noah and his family, and a male and female of every creature. Then He sent the great flood.

When the people of Sodom and Gomorrah wouldn't change their evil ways, He sent a fire storm to destroy both the cities and their inhabitants. Through the centuries God tried and tried to lead his people from a life of sin. He gave them the Ten

Commandments; through the prophets He told the people of his unhappiness. Still they continue to live in sin and idolatry. God had to be so grieved that he decided it was decision time.

He could have searched out those who were good and faithful and saved them while destroying all others. But, He had tried that and it hadn't worked for long. So, He sent his beloved Son to live amongst the peoples. In his ministry, Christ performed miracles, told parables to illustrate God's wishes for their lives, and most of all, taught that God is a God of love. He gave us the Eucharist as a remembrance of his sacrifice for forgiveness of our sins. This was all according to God's plan, but He knew that if his Son merely disappeared one day, the people would soon forget all He had taught them. God knew it needed something so dramatic that it could not and would not be forgotten.

God's plan was not a spur of the moment idea. Over 700 years earlier all of the events of Jesus's life on earth were foretold by the prophet Isaiah. God did not just say: "Well done, my Son" and bring him home. His plan began with the betrayal, then the whippings, the horror of the crucifixion, the death, and ultimately the resurrection. It ended with the glory of the Ascension. God wanted drama, and with His great powers, he got what he wanted. Without the drama, the life of Jesus could have become just a page or even just a footnote in history books. But... God's plan has worked. We have not forgotten. So yes, Christ did have to suffer and die.

It was God's powers that erased the upset that had caused me to lash out to Him. It was God's powers that erased the darkness in my heart. It was God's powers that led me to write and I firmly believe that the words I wrote were His words and my fingers were merely an agent.

He wanted me to understand completely and it worked. However, it was my prayer that had unleashed those mighty powers. When should we pray? I am convinced that this was perhaps one of the most important times in my life. It was as if something in me was saying: "Now.... now is the time". So, I listened to the still small voice speaking to me and prayed. It was time!

CHAPTER II

IT'S AN "I" CENTERED WORLD

WITH TODAY'S TECHNOLOGY, IT IS almost impossible not to see them; the ads and the promotions bombard us continually. We are told that whatever they are selling is bigger, better, and more efficient than the last model. We are told we must buy it now before the "special deal" ends.

The automobile industry is a prime example. We are shown a sleek, shiny car; of course it is their fanciest, highest priced model. All of its new features and amenities are detailed. Then comes "the deal"; we can buy this car and receive the same discount as their employees receive, a deal we must take advantage of right now because it will end soon. You look out the window and see "old faithful", the car that always starts, always gets you where you want to go and always back home again. It looked fine to you the last time you looked at it, but now it appears dented, worn and shabby. As you pick up your keys and head out the door, you are saying those words that are becoming all too familiar in this I-centered world...... "I need".

Today's fast food industry is another example. During a commercial break, a spokesman for a local eatery or fast food place begins to list the yummy ingredients in their new sandwich they are promoting. He goes on to say that the special introductory price is only good until Friday. Or, it may be an ad in the newspaper that catches your eye. Here the new sandwich is pictured along with a coupon for free fries if you purchase this new wonder by Friday. Your doctor's advice to cut down on fatty foods is fading fast; your mouth is watering; you are thinking: "surely one time won't hurt". So, you tear out the coupon and leave saying these words: "I want".

Magazines can be the worst offenders. Commercials only last a few moments; you can always change the channel or turn the TV off. Newspapers are thrown away or used to line the bird cage. But a magazine just hangs around and may be looked at over and over. For example: your favorite woman's magazine arrives and as you quickly flip through the pages you see a dress that catches your eye. From then on each time you pick up the magazine you seem to end up looking at that dress. Eventually you decide it is just what you should wear to your niece's wedding. As you look at it, you mentally take it off the model's body and attempt to put it on yours. Oops, there seems to be a problem; the model's 18 inch waist has increased by at least 6 inches; the slim hips are now amply padded; love handles and a tummy bulge are now evident; it just won't fit my figure. But, you say: "I wonder if it comes in my size?" as you turn the page.

On the next page you see an ad for the latest diet pills; pills that are guaranteed to take off 30 pounds in 30 days.

Or maybe it isn't an ad for pills; it may be an article for the latest fad diet that also promises an amazing weight loss. "This is my answer" you say; I have 3 months until the wedding and I can lose enough weight to fit in that dress. Forgotten are all the useless diet pills that were washed down the drain; forgotten are all the diets that were tried and given up on; forgotten is the fact that your niece loves you just as you are. All that remains are the desire to wear that dress and those same words……. "I need".

Our world is becoming more and more I-centered. The words I, me, and mine are taking over our lives and the words you, they and theirs are fast fading into the background. Less and less are people concerned with the wants and needs of others until they have satisfied their own. "I"-centered people can hurt other's feelings; "I"-centered people can step on others as they strive for self-advancement; "I"-centered people can have attributes that make them unpleasant even difficult to live with. People who focus on their own desires are happy only when they achieve them and then often for only a short time. -"I"-centered people can be conceited, often to the point that they feel the world is their apple and they deserve the biggest and best bite.

"I"-centered people do not stop to consider the cost when they give into their desires. The man who rushed out to buy the "amazing" new car wasn't thinking about what it would do to his bank account; wasn't thinking of what his family might have to do without; wasn't thinking about how all that extra power would make this car an expensive gas-guzzler. He was only thinking about himself. He was "I"-centered! The man who said "one time won't hurt" found that once he tasted the sandwich once wasn't enough. His cost wasn't just the food, ultimately it was his health. He also was "I"-centered. If the woman went ahead and bought the dress and/or the diet pills, her cost was money. But, she had another cost as well. She lost time; time spent on another fruitless effort to lose weight; time she surely could have found better uses for. She too was "I"-centered.

The companies responsible of the ads and commercials are doing their best to make sure this "I"-centered world continues. They pay big salaries to experts who create the ads that will catch and hold our attention; they pay millions of dollars to the TV networks, the newspapers, and the magazines. They know that far too many people today want the biggest, the best, and the latest model. They know the right words and/or pictures can change want into need, need into desire, and ultimately, desire into action. They know we can change the channel or go to the kitchen for a snack during the commercial; they know we can discard the newspapers and magazines. But, they know their ads will be repeated over and over because they have paid big bucks to make sure they will be. Most of all, they know that if people watch often enough and long enough, many will give in. They call this "good business". I call it temptation.

What is wrong with an "I"-centered world? It seems to work just fine. Big business is thriving, and we have more and better things that previous generations never even dreamed of. Imagine our lives without computers; we would have to spend hours writing letters. Imagine our lives without TV; we'd have to read the latest news (yesterday's at the best) in the paper. Imagine riding in a car without stereo or air conditioning. Imagine a car key that only locks and unlocks the doors and you need a crank to start the car. This is progress. How can it be wrong?

What is wrong is not the fact we have "things"; what is wrong is why we have acquired them. We don't fill our lives with most of these things out of need; we do it out of greed. The "I"-centered person will be happy with what they have only until the newer, bigger, better models come out. Then greed takes over. An "I"-centered person is no longer content to just keep up with the Joneses; they need to pass them up and leave them in the dust.

In Matthew 6:19 Jesus tells us: "Do not store up for yourselves treasures on earth". Paul understood the importance of these words because in Hebrews 13:5, he tells us: "Keep your lives free from the love of money, and be content with what you have". Neither Jesus nor Paul is telling us to do without and live in poverty; they are telling us we need to remove the greed from our lives.

In Ephesians 5:16, Paul tells us: "Let no one deceive you with empty words". When an ad or commercial sounds too good to be true, it probably is. If you are still tempted, recall the words Jesus gave us: "Lead us not into temptation, but deliver us from evil". This is exactly what God will do when we ask him for help.

The -"I"-centered person needs to change their focus, needs to stop looking inward and look outward to others. Most of all the "I"-centered person needs to look upward to God. In Peter 4:2, we are told: "Live for the rest of your earthly lives no longer by human desires but by the will of God". Long ago, when Moses asked God what his name was, God responded: "I am who I am". This is the only "I" that we should center our world on. We need to change our present "I"-centered world into a different one; we need to change it into a God-centered world.

Jesus has told us how to put his Father's great power to work in our lives. He began by telling us not to be greedy and fill our lives with "things". He went on to tell us not to worry about filling our needs because God knows them already and will take care of them. Finally, he tells us that God will give us all we need; we need only to ask.

Finally we find the magic words; words that can change our focus; words that can change our "I"-centered world into a God-centered one. They are magic words that will give us access to the power we need; the power that will give us the strength to resist the temptation we find in the commercials; the power to resist torturing ourselves with yet another diet; the power to say no to that delicious looking sandwich we know we shouldn't have.

Jesus tells us we need only to ask God for help. I feel the word "ask" should be written in capital letters. It is important, it is vital; it is our approach to God's powers. We need to ask; by no means should we ever order God to put his powers to work for us. No one tells God what to do! He doesn't take orders, He gives them. Jesus understood this when He said: "Not my will but Thy will be done".

God will help us only when we ask; only when we humble ourselves and ask in prayer. This is why this chapter is in my book on prayer. It had started out to be a chapter in the section entitled "Why", but as I wrote I moved it to "when". I felt it belongs here because it shows over and over when we should pray. Meal times, bed times, special times we set aside for conversation with God, all these are important times when we should pray. But they are not the only times!

We need to pray WHEN we need the wisdom to understand that our bodies are a gift created by God and thus they are not ours to do with as we wish. We need to pray WHEN we begin to weaken and give into temptation. We need to pray WHEN we acknowledge that our "I"-centered world needs to change. We need to pray WHEN we realize it can only change through God and his power. We need to pray WHEN we need to ask God for his help. We need to pray, and pray, and pray some more, never mind worrying when, just do it!

CHAPTER III

THE BARREN
PRAYER TIMES

One day I sought a quiet place
        To spend some time in prayer.
Only to feel my words bounce back
        As if a wall were there.
Then came a sense of darkness
        Like the day had turned to night;
I could have turned on all the lamps
        But that wouldn't restore the light.
I felt an dreadful emptiness,
        As if no one was there.
Oh, where has everyone gone,
        Is there not anyone to care?
I began to feel a burning thirst.
        Not a thirst from lack of water;
It was a thirst that can only be felt
        While searching for the Father.
I know God has a plan for me
        But I'm puzzled what to do;

Is this God's testing of my faith,
  Or the start of something new?
So, I won't spend time in worry,
  In fear, nor in despair;
Tho I cannot feel His presence now,
  I know God still is there.

THE BARREN PRAYER TIME

WHEN SHOULD WE PRAY? HAVE you ever encountered an occasion when you are ready for a time of prayer and nothing happens? You are alone, you have no unfinished tasks to distract you; you have been reading scripture and have set the Bible aside. You normally would begin to pray, but this time it is as if your mind has shut down. There are no words forthcoming. Not only are you at a loss for words, your mind seems to be a complete blank. What is going on you wonder; this is not normal. Is God unhappy with me for some reason and is shutting me out? You continue to sit and wonder as time passes with no change.

Finally your voice returns and you begin to speak, but not much has changed. Now it feels as if a wall is between you and the Lord, and your words are just bouncing back at you. Your distress grows as you realize that not only can you not feel God's presence, He appears not to be listening either.

Not only do you not feel the Father's presence, but the Son appears to be missing also. Although in John 8:12, Jesus says: "I am the light of the world. Whoever follows me will never walk in darkness but will have the light of life", you feel only darkness in your soul.

This is perhaps one of the most difficult times of all in a believer's life. You have devoted your life to following God's desires. Day after day you spend time in conversation with him, so why can you not communicate today? It is not for lack of trying though. You wait and wait; you keep trying to pray but nothing is the same.

You cannot understand what is happening. There is no joy, only darkness and despair. Your heart feels as barren as the Sahara Desert. You feel much as David had to when in Psalm 22:1 he said: "My God, my God, why have you forsaken me?" You can only wonder; has God turned his back on me? Did He put up that wall? Does He no longer care? These are terrible thoughts, but you cannot seem to turn them off. If it were not for the darkness and emptiness, they are thoughts you probably would never entertain. Such thoughts would never come because you would know they were not true. The purpose of the ministry of Jesus was to teach us that God is not a God of revenge; He is a God of love; a love that has no boundaries. Also Jesus taught us that God will always be with us; He will never turn away; He will not desert us.

When should we pray? What to do, what to do? Should you keep praying in hopes that the wall, like the wall of Jericho, will come tumbling down? Should you keep praying in hopes that the darkness will end and joy will return? Should you keep praying, or are you just wasting your time? We tend to measure our love for God by how and what we feel; but He does not work that way. What we call a barren time of darkness He calls a time of fruitfulness. What time we may feel has been wasted,

He feels is time well spent. He, after all is God, and He sees things not as we do but as He does.

If only you knew the cause of the problem, perhaps you could find the answer to why it is happening. But, how can you find the cause? Under most circumstances when you have a problem, you can ask God for help and He will lead you to an answer. Now it appears that you are on your own and you are at a loss for ideas.

You begin to wonder if perhaps God is testing your faith; or is this possibly the beginning of a new part of His plan for your life. If this is the cause, you may never fully know because, as Paul wrote in 1Corinthinians 2:9: "No eye has seen, no ear has heard, no mind has conceived what God has prepared for those who love him."

Then you begin to wonder anew if you yourself could be the cause. Is there something from long ago hidden so deep in your heart that even you have forgotten about it? If so, remember that God knows our every secret, no matter how well hidden it is. If so, it would be time to bring it to light and ask for forgiveness. Have you recently done something wrong and have not asked for forgiveness? If and when this happens the Holy Spirit will give your conscience a nudge and will continue to do so until you ask.

You are feeling a sense of loss; you believe you have lost all communication with the Father. But, what may God be feeling during your time of darkness? Although you feel as if your words are echoing back to you, He is hearing them.

When we feel nothing but emptiness we stir the heart of God. David knew this as over and over in the Psalms he cries out to the Lord for compassion when he feels a time of barrenness. Any prayer, even a very short one given in a time of emptiness is not fruitless to God. Even an attempt to pray when nothing seems to be forthcoming is felt by Him. Try as we may, in our quest for complete intimacy with God, we may and probably will encounter these times of darkness. As long as we remember the words in Isaiah 41:10, "Do not be dismayed for I am your God", we not despair. We will know that He understands, He loves us, and this darkness will pass and the joy and the closeness will return. We need only to have patience and to believe.

When should we pray? Right now, as I finish this chapter sounds like a good time to me. I am going to pray; will you join me?

PART IV

WHERE SHOULD WE PRAY?

"Whenever you pray, go into your room and shut the
door and pray to your Father who is in secret; and
your Father who sees in secret will reward you."
Matthew 6:6

WHERE SHOULD WE PRAY?

WHERE SHOULD WE PRAY? DOES God care where we are when we speak to Him? Would He ever tell us to wait to begin our prayers until we move to a better location? Of course not! The fact that we are praying is all that matters to Him.

Where should we pray? Jesus says we should not be hypocrites as we pray in church or at street corners. He isn't telling us not to pray in church, course we should. He isn't telling us not to pray in public; there is nothing wrong with doing that either. I believe what He is telling us is not to do so in a manner so ostentatiously that we draw attention to ourselves; not to make a show of our piety, of our righteousness, of our devotion.

Where should we pray? In Matthew 6:6, Jesus tells us to go into our room, shut the door, and pray in secret. However, the Gospels recount many times when Jesus prayed; on a mountain top, in the upper room, in Gethsemane, even on the cross. But, no where does it say he went into a room by himself to pray. So, why does Jesus tell us to do something He did not do himself? I believe He is just telling us to pray somewhere with no distractions.

Before Jesus died for our sins, only one high priest could be in God's presence. That high priest could only be in God's presence once a year. The high priest could only be in God's presence in the Most Holy Place. However, after Jesus died for our sins, anyone can be in God's presence. You can be in God's presence anytime. You can be in God's presence anywhere.

CHAPTER 1

IT'S BEDTIME

WHERE SHOULD WE PRAY? ONE of my earliest memories is kneeling at my bedside each evening to pray. I would recite a simple, memorized prayer and then add blessings for others. My list always included my parents, my grandparents, aunts and uncles, best friends, and occasionally some new person. I remember that I had just watched one of her earlier movies, so I added Shirley Temple's name to the list that night.

I still pray at the side of my bed, but no longer on my knees. As I have grown older, so have my bones and joints. As a result, if I now kneel down, I cannot get back up without help. Therefore, I now keep a chair next to my bed and I sit there while I pray. Other than the change of position, I still do end my day in prayer as I speak whatever words my heart tells me to say. A couple years ago I did add something, something that brings me comfort that brings me peace. What is that, you say? It is just 7 words, ordinary words, but apparently very special words to God. These words are: "I love you, my Father; good night". Having said them, sleep comes quickly and easily.

Where should we pray? Of course at the bedside is a perfect place. It doesn't matter whether you kneel, sit, or even stand. God has given you another day on earth and now it is almost over. It may have been a good day or a bad one, but it was a day of your life, so why not show your gratitude. The day was filled with gifts from the Lord, gifts that need to be acknowledged, gifts we need to say thank you for. Don't you feel bad when you give someone a gift and they just walk away? I am sure your feelings are hurt. But, God has feelings too and I don't believe you want to hurt the Lord. So, take the time to empty your heart of things it is carrying; take the time to say thank you for all his blessings; take time to say good night to the Father. You won't be sorry. Your sleep will be peaceful for sure.

CHAPTER 2

IT'S TIME TO EAT

WHERE SHOULD WE PRAY? AGAIN one of my childhood memories is that of learning the simple prayer: "God is great, God is good, and we thank Him for our food". Yes, this is a simple prayer but at the same time it is a complete one. It includes an acknowledgement of His supremacy; it includes praise; it includes our gratitude for the food we are about to receive. This prayer was always offered by a family member before each meal.

We may use this simple prayer, or we may use words of our own, but the family table definitely is one place we should pray. Then, what about other tables in other places? Should we also pray there? Always a prayer is given before a public luncheon or dinner and at all times before a church meal. So yes, in cases like these we should say a prayer.

But what if you have been invited to someone's home for a meal? Should you pray there also? Perhaps everyone is seated, the food is on the table, and people are beginning to fill their plates. At this moment you realize that no one has offered a prayer. So, what should you do? As I see it, you have three choices. First, you could ask the host or hostess for permission to pray; second, you could just start to pray out loud; or, third, you could just pray by yourself silently.

If you were to start to pray aloud, it can have several different results. It could be disruptive; it could cause people to stop filling their plates to see who is talking and to whom; it could cause conversations to end so people can hear what you are saying. Also, it may cause the host and/or the hostess to be embarrassed. However, the upside to just starting to pray is that you have caught some of the people's attention, some are listening, and some may even feel the need join you in prayer.

If you have found that no one seems inclined to pray, you may at this time ask permission to do so. This too can bring about mixed responses. Hopefully you will be told: "Please do so". Then again, with less enthusiasm, you may be told: "I guess it will be alright, but please make it short so the food doesn't get cold". The worst response you could get would be something like: "We never do pray, so we'd rather you didn't either".

Whether you just start to pray aloud, ask permission, or pray silently, it has to be your decision to make. This decision can depend of a number of things. You may be at a small informal gathering, at a large formal dinner party, or at something somewhere in between. The people may be family members, good friends, or mere acquaintances. You may be seated at a kitchen tables, using the everyday dishes or at a large formal dining table set with china and crystal. But, wherever you are and whoever is there with you, it is still your decision to make.

Where should we pray? What if you're not in a home and are about to eat in a restaurant? Do you feel free to pray there, or are you afraid to draw the attention of other diners? Do you feel that to do so would be not obeying Jesus' words in Matthew 6:5? Why do you think that other diners who are either busy talking or eating would even notice what you are doing?

I recall an incident that happened some time ago. I was traveling and one morning I stopped for breakfast in a diner in a small town. I was waiting for my food to come when I noticed a young man arriving. He went to a table next to mine and sat down facing me. He looked around for a moment and then held up two fingers. He picked up a book and began to read it. I could see the title; it was the Holy Bible he was reading.

About this time my food arrived but I barely noticed it; I was too fascinated. Who is this man I wondered? Is he one of the new era Christians I had heard about, or is he perhaps a student in a seminary? Then his food arrived, he set the book aside, bowed his head, and both his lips and fingers began to move. Suddenly I realized three things; I was being rude by staring; my food had arrived, and it was now cold. There are few things I dislike more than eating cold fried eggs, so I decided to forego the meal and leave. But, I found I couldn't just leave. I had to know who this man was. So, as I paid the bill, I asked the waitress and she said he comes in almost every day and, although he can talk, he never says a word. He is an instructor at the local school for the deaf and he lets his fingers do the talking for him. Of course, I realized, he was using sign language to pray.

From that day on if I might hesitate to pray before eating out, I would remember that this stranger had taught me an important lesson. I could, of course use sign language as he did, but I have never learned how to do so. I could speak very softly, could just whisper words, or even could merely think them. What was the lesson I learned that day? It is…if there's a will, there's a way. It is up to me!

Why is praying before a meal so important? The Bible tells us of several occasions when Jesus did so; before the feedings of the multitude and before the meal in the upper room, for example. If Jesus did so, why not do so also. Since He showed us over and over what we should do, could his actions be another lesson he gave us?

The Bible is filled with passages where we are told to pray. Jesus told us to as did Paul. Isaiah also told us to pray and so did David many, many times. In Thessalonians 5:18, Paul tells us: "Give thanks in all circumstances for this is the will of God in Jesus Christ for you". In today's world millions are starving, but we have food before us. So, if we are told to pray and told to give thanks, why not do so before we eat what the Lord has provided for us.

CHAPTER 3

THE GREAT OUTDOORS

A GIFT OF GLORY

I took a walk this morning
    As the sun began to show;
My eyes were drawn upwards
    To the clouds that seemed to glow.
The sky was mostly cloud filled,
    Showed some bits of blue so bold;
The clouds were either gray or white,
    But, all sun-tinged with gold.
My heart was filled with wonder
    At the glory there to see;
I knew it was a gift from God,
    A gift prepared for me.
So, I raised my eyes to heaven,
    Lifted up my voice in prayer;
I thanked the Lord for His wondrous gift.
    And for His loving care.

WHERE SHOULD WE PRAY? MUST we be within four walls or can we open the door and go outside? Jesus often prayed outdoors; He prayed by the shore, on the mountain top, in the Garden of Gethsemane, even on the cross. He didn't feel the need for shelter when he prayed, so why should we?

Where should we pray? You could go outside at different times of the year. Whether it is rainy, windy or sunny, spring presents an endless period of awakenings and development. Summer may be hot but you can find relief in the shade of a tree or in the cool waters of a lake or stream. Fall presents a kaleidoscope of colors as the plants change from green to a glorious array of hues. Depending on where you live, winter is unique. In some areas the only change may be just a slight lowering of the temperature. Other areas can get quite cold, often mighty cold to be sure. But, the cold has a purpose. It keeps the snow from melting, the snow which is a God-given blanket covering the earth while it sleeps until it awakens in the spring. The same places can look different in each area and in each season, so don't just pick a favorite time or place; try them all.

The list of places you could go to is endless. The simplest would be to just go out into your own yard if you have one. Or, you could go to a city or a state park, the beach or a forest preserve. You could go at different times of the day. At early morning or in the evening are special times; then you can watch the full glory of the sun rising or setting. Of course these are all local sites or at least ones just a short bit away. Any or all of them will offer excellent places to observe the Lord's handiwork. They are great places to pray.

I have moved several times; from the mid-west to southern California, to Maine, back to the mid-west, and finally back to California. From gently rolling hills, to towering mountains, to a rocky coastline, I was constantly in awe at the variety of places that God had created and, almost as if it was pre-arranged, I would find the perfect place to spend time in praise and gratitude for God's handiwork., I truly enjoyed short jaunts, as each turn of the road could present a new vista and a new opportunity for prayer. However, I also sometimes traveled distances. I love to board a plane, a train, a bus, or best of all, just climb behind the wheel of my car and take off for new places.

When I traveled by car I would usually go around this country visiting new and different places. I preferred this mode of travel because then I could stop whenever I wanted and go wherever I wished. Occasionally I would have a definite destination; maybe it would be a place I had heard about or read about and was intrigued to see. But, mostly I like to just pick a road and set out. I tended to travel at a slow rate, ignoring the high-speed super highways, while admiring the ever-changing panorama. Sometimes, for no special reason and with no fore-thought, I would come to a cross-road and turn onto it. I was rarely sorry I did it because I usually would come to a new and unique place to pray.

One time I came to a quaint vine-covered country church with a little cemetery next to it. Nearest to the road was a well-weathered cross. Obviously it was quite old, but it was also apparent that someone cared, because the grave was well tended and flowers were growing at the foot of the old cross. I began to pray and suddenly found myself trying to sing the lovely hymn: "The Old Rugged Cross". Although I cannot carry a tune very well, I did know all the words and I am sure that God understood and appreciated the effort I made.

Another time one of the little roads led me into a heavily wooded area. The road wound and twisted through the trees until it suddenly ended at a little clearing. I saw that someone had placed a little rustic bench in the clearing. It faced a lovely little waterfall. As if it were timed, just as I sat down on the bench, a ray of sunlight came through the trees and lit the waterfall. Immediately the spray began to sparkle like diamonds. Somehow, I knew that God had led me to this spot and with his great powers had brought about this glorious spectacle. The beauty and serenity of the place presented the perfect place for prayer; so, I began to pray. Wouldn't you have if you were there?

I loved those car trips, but a plane or train was needed if I had to go a great distance in a relatively short time. However, either altitude and/or speed made it difficult to view God's handiworks we were passing. These modes of transportation are merely a means to an end, but they can still present prayer opportunities. I have found I could pray for the parents of a fussy child, could pray for the health of a passenger who kept coughing, and of course, would pray for a safe journey.

Twice I have flown across the Atlantic. The first time I went to Scandinavia. I did enjoy touring Sweden and Denmark; each presented a totally different landscaper and, therefore, totally different opportunities for prayer.

But, it was Norway that captured my heart. With every turn of the road new evidence of God's awesome works appeared. Norway is called the land of midnight sun for good reason; I was there in July and I truly believe that each day had 23 hours and 59 minutes of sunshine. Possibly due to this fact, I recall an incident when I got a bit imaginative. We were about half way through our tour and for several days our bus had been passing clear blue lakes and fast moving streams. I was standing on the shore of a lovely fjord ringed by tall snow-capped mountains when I began to wonder how all this beauty came about. Did God look down one day and say to himself: "Oh my, all that sunshine is melting the glaciers. I must prepare a place for all that water". Then, did he reach down, make thumb-prints for lakes, make twisting lines for rivers, and where these lines met, press hard with his mighty middle finger, deepening a valley and forming a fjord to hold the waters? Oh how can I think such things I thought, but then again, who knows. It could have happened that way. It was at this point I fell to my knees and, ignoring the fanciful thoughts and the other travelers with me; I thanked the Lord for the glory and majesty of it all.

There was another thing that made a deep impression on me in Norway. I found the whole country to be spotless. There was no trash, no litter to be found anywhere. Also, everywhere we went we saw churches; even the tiniest towns had one and usually the town was built around it, making it the center. From these two facts I believe that people knew who had created this lovely land, knew they were meant to care for it, and knew they had to say thank you to the Lord. It appears that it is truly a nation that loves, honors, and obeys God. What better place could one find to inspire prayer?

My second trip abroad was to the alpine region of central Europe. Here I found Switzerland to be much the same as Norway. The only exception, since it is land-locked, was the absence of the fjords. Austria also was much alike except that it too had no fjords and had much more flat land. The real high-light of this trip came when we visited the small village of Oberamergau deep in the Alps of southern Germany. Every ten years this village presents the Passion Play in gratitude for God sparing its people from the plague. I find it hard to believe that anyone who had sat through this day-long awesome presentation would not feel the need to pray. I know that in the evening afterwards I found a quiet place and I prayed, and prayed, and then I prayed some more.

I realize this chapter has kept growing longer and longer. But, I do seem to have an innate ability to make a short story long. However, in this case it was done for a purpose. It was done to show that there are innumerable places to pray. It was done in the hope that couch potatoes would turn off the TV and go outside their homes. It was done in the hope that people who seldom wander far from their homes will be inspired to do so and thus see more and more of God's handiwork. It was done in the hope that, if I have inspired people to travel, I have also inspired them to pray.

CHAPTER 4

IT'S TIME TO VISIT

I asked the Lord to bless you
    As I prayed for you today.
To guide you and protect you
    As you go along your way.
Hs love is always with you
    His promises always true.
You know in all your struggles that
    He will see you through.
So, when the road you're traveling
    Seems difficult at best,
Take a moment, say a prayer
    And God will do the rest.

WHERE SHOULD WE PRAY? IF you thought I had run out of suggested places for prayer, you were wrong. True, I had only just mentioned the church because I felt it was obvious that we should pray there. However, I do have another idea that can offer prayer opportunities.

I am sure all of you have had an occasion to pay a visit to someone, somewhere, at some time. Do you know someone who, perhaps due to age, to infirmity, or to illness, is unable to leave their home? Have you ever been house-bound, even for a short time? I was, after suffering a mild stroke. The first day I enjoyed the peace and quiet. The second day I had enough of the quiet so I turned on the TV to find only soap operas and tempestuous talk shows. Neither was to my liking so I shut it off and decided to read, but I discovered I had already read all of the books I had.

Now, I had never been one to just sit idly. If I wasn't hopping in my car and going somewhere, most often to a church function or service, I was doing some kind of work with my hands. I loved to solve puzzles; I would spend many hours knitting, crocheting, or embroidering items for sale at church bazaars or for gifts for my family. But, the stroke had affected my hands somewhat so these activities were out of the question for the time being. Use of the car was completely gone, so I did what was previously unthinkable for me; I just sat.

I did have visitors. The visiting nurse came twice a week, but she was very quick, efficient and seldom stayed long. It was the second visitor or visitors that quickly became the high-light of each day. For a number of years I had delivered meals on wheels and now I was receiving them. Each day I would sit and anxiously watch the clock, waiting for the knock on the door and the cheerful call: "Meals on wheels". Normally these deliveries were made quickly so that each recipient would receive their food while it was still hot. However, I was the last one on the route and I knew most of the people, so once they had put the food on the table, they would often give me a hug and spend a few minutes talking to me. These few minutes of human contact brightened my day.

I also heard from friends. Usually they would call me on the phone and say they were going to come for a visit. But, often then the "buts and maybes" began. But I have a meeting today; have an appointment tomorrow, but maybe I can make it the next day. These were some of them, but the biggest "but" of all came when we got a massive snow storm and it became too hazardous to drive. Don't misunderstand me; I did have visitors other than the nurse and the ones delivering the meals. My church had a service called: "Food for Friends". I only got Meals on Wheels on week days, so they brought me dinners on the weekends and even an occasional evening meal during the week. Most of the time they would stay for a while and visit; but they always stayed long enough for a prayer.

Now I don't mean to complain about the excuses; I realized their lives were just as busy as mine had been. But, they did care enough to call and very often did find time to drop in for a visit, even a short one. But, they almost always did offer a prayer and almost always said: "God bless you", a simple but much appreciated prayer.

In the beginning I said that visiting a shut-in could be a prayer opportunity; in fact, it should be. I did have three visitors who definitely understood this fact. We would talk for a few minutes and then they would say: "Shall we pray?" It was what followed these words that taught me a lesson I have not forgotten and I pray each of you will remember it also. Before starting to pray they would take hold of my hands and at that moment an amazing feeling would come over me. My heart would seem to open and my whole being would feel warm and alert. Maybe it was the contact with another person, but I feel there was another reason. I believe Jesus gave the reason in Matthew 18:20, when He said: "For where two or more are gathered in my name, I am there among them". When we joined our hands, we were gathered in his name and, true to his words, He was there. It had to be his presence I was feeling.

Where should we pray? Everything I have talked about so far has been in reference to the home-bound. There are others who are house-bound, but not in their own homes. My mother lived in an assisted living home for the last years of her life and, although she admitted she was no longer safe living alone, she was not really happy there. Although she had brought her own bed, her favorite easy chair, and even her beloved African violets, it just wasn't the same. Each time I came to visit her, within minutes she would begin her list of complaints. Many of them were just petty things, some were downright ridiculous, and almost all were repeats from the last time I visited her. Was a visit to her a prayer opportunity? Most definitely they were, in fact before too many visits they became multiple opportunities.

Mom was in her 90's and had become crotchety and very self-centered. She wanted everything her way and was quick to complain when it wasn't. Her complaints were not only about the help, they were also about me. Mostly it was that I didn't come often enough and didn't stay long enough when I did come. When I said I stayed long enough to talk and often to play a game or two, she said it wasn't long enough. When I said I did come every other day and when I didn't come it was because I was busy at church, she said that since I cared more for the church than for her, I should move my bed into the church and live there.

Each time I set out to visit her I had to wonder how I would be greeted that day. Would she be wearing a smile, a frown, or a scowl? I had only a 5 minute drive and I usually spent those minutes in prayer. This was my first opportunity for prayer as I prayed for patience. The second and main opportunity would come near the end of the visit. At this time I would ask mom to join me in a prayer. Normally she would sit quietly and listen as I prayed, but one day she did something very uncharacteristic of her. She suddenly interrupted my prayer and told me to tell God to teach those girls how to make her bed properly and how to cook her food the way she likes it.

This was the outburst that caused the third prayer opportunity that day. I had been so astonished that I didn't even finish the prayer. I just told my mom that it was wrong to interrupt a prayer like that and I told her so very loudly and angrily. Then I just walked out and drove home. This time the 5 minute drive was spent in prayer as I asked God's forgiveness.

Some of you may also have a family member or friend living in an assisted living home. Even if you know no one, you could still visit. Some of the residents have no one living close and they do get lonely. I am sure you can find such facilities somewhere near you, and if you call or drop in they will be happy to introduce you to someone who would love to have a visitor. This person would probably be quite willing to talk to you. They might talk about their family, their friends, where they used to live, and possibly tell stories of things they have done and places they have gone to. You could also tell them things about yourself and, even though you have been complete strangers, a friendship may begin. One thing though, before you leave be sure to offer to pray, I doubt they will say no.

Where should we pray? Perhaps a person is unable to reside anywhere but in a nursing home. They too may be lonely, may be unhappy just being there. I am sure they would love a visit just as the ones in assisting living did. The only difference I can see is that, due to illness or infirmity, you may have to make the visit short. It could be just a few words of greeting, a prayer or just a short prayer; but for sure, make it a prayer.

Where should we pray? You may know someone who has had an accident, had surgery, or had a heart attack or stroke. They are in a hospital and if they are conscious, surely would appreciate a visit. Of course the doctor comes in and nurses pop in often for one reason or another. But, I am sure the patient will appreciate a visitor who isn't carrying pills to be taken and doesn't hold a needle for a blood draw. They need someone who just wants to visit. They will probably welcome the visit, but keep the visit friendly, keep it cheerful, and since they will tire easily, keep it short. Yes, do not stay too long, but be sure to stay long enough for a prayer.

Where should we pray? The shut-ins, the ill or injured, the elderly, or the infirm all will welcome a visit and a prayer. So, what about someone who is depressed? Was a recent divorce involved? Divorce can be traumatic for the man, but it can be the woman who suffers the most. No longer is there someone to warm her feet at night; no longer is there someone to do odd jobs or fix things around the home; no longer is there someone to bring home a paycheck each week.

If the marriage had ended in a bitter fight, the woman may enjoy the peaceful life for a while. Then problems begin to appear and pile up and also loneliness begins to set in. It may not be long before she is depressed and this is an unhappy thing. Of course, there can be many causes for depression other than divorce; finances, family problems, or even a prolonged illness for example. No matter what started it, the result is the same. The first thing normally a depressed person does is to withdraw, withdraw from everything and from everyone.

I am not a trained counselor; I have never claimed to be one, and I never will. But, I do know that a person in depression can be reached and can be helped. There is one thing that you should never do, never use pressure because that could just make them withdraw even more. It undoubtedly was pressure of one kind or another that started it all so adding more pressure is a bad idea. One other thing you should not do is to give up trying to make contact.

What you do need to do is to persevere. If one method isn't working, try another way, just as long as you keep trying. You may not see success over night, it may take a long time, and so have patience. Whatever you do, be sure to do it with love. They may not admit it or even realize it, but they need to know that someone cares. You need to keep trying, but even more important, you need to keep praying. Although you may not be able to pray with the person, you absolutely can and should pray for them. God understands the problems. He knows what to do; He just needs someone to ask him for help. So, don't hesitate, ask, and he will guide you in every step along the way. This is his promise.

Where should we pray? I say anywhere and everywhere that an opportunity appears, especially with those who because of one reason or another are in need of prayer.

CHAPTER 5

IT'S TIME FOR SORROW

Your loved one now has gone away,
    Is with the Lord you know.
The suffering done, the soul at peace,
    In His arms now at rest.
Your heart is sore, the ache is real,
    You raise you voice and pray,
I trust in You to ease my pain,
    Oh God, please give me rest.
Your eyes still cry, your soul needs peace,
    You know He hears your prayers.
You know God's love will heal the hurt,
    For your loved one's home at last.

WHERE SHOULD WE PRAY? THERE has been a death; it may be a family member, a neighbor, a friend, or maybe even a complete stranger. In your heart you know it is a time for prayer, but where should you pray is the question. But it is not the only question, since when is also important. At this point please bear with me as I again turn to a personal experience.

My mother was approaching 100 years of age. She had suffered a stroke and then a massive heart attack and was now in the hospital. My sister and I, along with my brother and family were in the room with mom, but she was unconscious and didn't know we were there. Finally we left to get some rest, but around 5am the next morning, the hospital called each of us and said we should come now. Mom looked the same as when we left; still lying quietly and appearing to be unconscious. Immediately three things Jesus had told us came to my mind: "In my Father's house are many dwelling places", "I go to prepare a place for you", and "Ask and it will be given you". I knew then what I had to do, so I went down the hall to the little chapel and began to pray: "Heavenly Father, my mom has had a long life, she has had a good life, but now she is tired. If it is your will, please hold her hand and take her home".

I had just finished the prayer when I felt an urgent need to return to mom's room. As soon as I entered, my mom's hand rose and she gave a big sigh, not a sigh of pain or discomfort, but rather a sigh of contentment. I knew then that God had answered my prayer; He had taken her home and she was now at peace. This had been my first prayer of the day and it was quickly followed by the second one as I expressed my gratitude.

It was the day of the funeral. Everyone that wished to do so had said good-bye to mom and finally the service began. Everything proceeded as planned with one exception; pastor knew that mom loved to listen to the handbells play, so he had arranged for one of the ringers to play a medley of hymns. I am sure mom was listening and was smiling with pleasure.

Now, it was time for me to give the eulogy and I had no idea what I was going to say. As I slowly made my way to the front of the sanctuary, I prayed for help, but it was more of a plea than a request. I stood there in a panic; my knees were shaking; my mind was a blank; I knew I was about to make a fool of myself. It was at that moment that I began to speak. At no time did I have to stop to decide what to say next, the words just came; words that recounted memories; words that gave testimony to the wonderful mother and the special person she had been. Tears were flowing as I finished and I barely made it back to my seat. After the service people told me that I had given a wonderful tribute to my mom. But I knew better; although I had spoken the words, I had not done it alone. I knew the words had passed from the loving heart of God to my lips; I knew He had once again answered my prayer.

Yes, He had answered when he knew the time was right and what did I do in the meanwhile? Did I wait patiently for his help or did I panic? When I recalled Christ's words in Matthew 14:32: "You of little faith, why did you doubt?" I realized what I had done. My faith had wavered; I had doubted that God was going to help so I panicked. I was horrified at what I had done. I knew what I had to do, so I took off by myself to find a quiet place, a place where I could pray. I offered no excuses for what I had done as, with a heavy heart, I began to pray. It was when I begged God's forgiveness for my lapse that Jesus' words in Matthew 7:7: "Ask and you shall receive" came true. The heaviness in my heart was gone and I knew instantly that forgiveness was mine.

Where should we pray? I believe I have already shown that it can be anywhere and everywhere and anytime. What really matters is the prayer itself. There is one thing I suggest you always keep in mind; the promise that Jesus made in Matthew 11:28: "Come to me, all you that are weary and heavy-laden and I will give you rest". This is the keystone of our faith; but what many don't seem to realize is that His promise of rest is given for the bereaved as well as for the deceased. I know this fact was in my mind when I wrote the poem given at the cover page of this chapter. I have made many copies of it and now enclose one with each condolence card I send. If you like that idea, feel free to make your own copies and do the same.

Where should we pray? If you still feel the need to ask that question, perhaps you need to go back and read all of this section again. I do believe I have covered the "where's", the "when's", and the "why's" of every conceivable situation is could think of. If you feel I missed something, I apologize.

Where should we pray? Again I say, if you feel the need to pray and you stop to ask if you are in the right place, you are just wasting time. There is no wrong place to pray! Wherever you are is the right place, so go ahead and pray. God is waiting to hear from you.

PART V

HOW SHOULD WE PRAY?

HOW SHOULD WE PRAY?

HOW SHOULD WE PRAY? Do you feel there is a proper position? How do you pray? Do you kneel, stand, sit, or whatever position you are in as you begin? What is the proper position? The Bible recounts many positions. Peter knelt before the Lord. Nehemiah sat down. Elijah put his face between his knees. Abraham prostrated himself. Paul witnessed early believers lifting up their hands. So, what is right and is there really a right position or a wrong one? Does it matter along as you are enabled to respond to the presence of God?

CHAPTER 1

IS THERE A PROPER BODY POSITION FOR PRAYER?

"IN THE BEGINNING WAS THE Word". These words begin the Gospel of John and for the most part, believers also have a beginning with a word. This was a word not given by the Lord or an Apostle, it was a word given to them by a parent at a very early age. Of course this word is prayer. We learn it when we are taught to end our days by kneeling with bowed head and closed eyes besides our beds and then reciting a simple prayer. This is an activity and a prayer position first used in childhood. But, now we are adults. For some people, kneeling can be uncomfortable, can be painful, maybe can even be impossible. This is especially true for the elderly and for those who are physically handicapped in some way.

There are some denominations that believe we should kneel. Often a low bench or stool is provided, but some just kneel on the bare floor. There are also many who stand for prayer. So, the question remains: do we or should we kneel while we pray?

At times I do kneel to pray. Now, I am not a believer in horoscopes; however for years those who do follow these things have told me that I am a Leo and as such I am a leader. I have no idea if there is any validity to these beliefs, but I do know I have always had a strong tendency to be bossy. I would propose a thought or idea and would insist I was right. How egotistical of me! This lack of humility became a major stumbling block in my road to salvation. No matter how hard I tried, this same old habit would reappear. Each time I would pray for forgiveness and I would be okay for a while, but only for a while. Then one day I was kneeling as I prayed and I made an amazing discovery. Kneeling had put me in an attitude of humility. Kneeling had helped me realize the supremacy of the one I was speaking to. Kneeling had done away with most distractions; not much is visible from this lowly position. Now, if that old habit reappears or I feel a deep need for help, I kneel in humility. So, one answer to the question is yes, it is okay to kneel while praying, but it is not necessarily the only position to use.

Since kneeling is not the only position to pray, what other positions may we use? Speaking from personal experience, I normally begin my day seated in my comfortable favorite chair. In the past I would sit in a wicker lawn chair on my covered front porch. While seated, I read scripture and then I pray. Seated in my car, as I drive I pray as I express praise and gratitude for all that my eyes behold. I have prayed for a safe flight while seated on an airplane. I have even felt the need to pray while seated in a bath tub. Therefore, I can see no reason that along with kneeling, sitting is also a proper position for prayer.

In many churches, as in the one I attend, we stand for a time of prayer. I find that while I am standing, I feel a sense of reverence. I feel this is an acknowledgement of the supremacy of the one being spoken to. There are also other times I stand as I pray. One of these is while I am doing house work as then I voice my gratitude for all the possessions. Another time is while I am preparing a meal and I thank God for the bounty of foods I have.

If kneeling, sitting, and standing can be proper positions, what about while lying down? At the end of a hard day your back may ache, your legs and/or arms may feel leaden and nothing will make you feel better than to just stretch out and rest. You are now relaxing and at ease so why waste this time? What better use of this time than to pray? On occasion I find myself praying after I am already snug in bed at night. Even though I had finished my day with prayer, I might suddenly realize I have more to say to God. No, I do not get up and kneel beside the bed nor do I put on a robe and move out to my favorite chair. I remain as I am, comfortable under the covers and I pray. I have on occasion come wide awake during the wee hours of the night and find that something I didn't even realize was a problem was now troubling me. I could have merely said to myself, "I'll worry about that in the morning". However, I have tried that and found that sleep would not return. I needed to pray now, not later. I need to ask God's help with whatever has disturbed my sleep. Only then will I find peace and return to sleep.

One day I told my pastor how I had been praying and he interrupted me by saying: "That is not really prayer, it is just conversation". Then he was quiet for a few minutes after which he said: "I was wrong. It is prayer, prayer in its most basic form, prayer coming straight from a caring heart". Sometime after this our study group was introduced to a book which detailed the value of this very form of prayer. What more can I say? Obviously it doesn't matter to God what position we are in, he will listen, and he will answer our prayers.

Now, I will speak a bit about specific parts of the body. From early childhood we were taught we should close our eyes while praying and most people still hold this to be true. Of course there are several reasons for doing this. We are mere humans and as such we are easily distracted. A fussy child, the shuffle of feet, a bird passing a window; all of these plus many, many more things can distract us if our eyes are open. It is only human to take a peak. However, when the eyes are closed, the back of the eyelids are blank, as blank as a TV screen when the power is turned off. There is nothing to see, no distraction is visible when our eyes are closed.

I will admit that sometimes I pray with open eyes. In the front of my church is a lovely picture of Christ and my former church had a large back-lit cross. I often find my eyes drawn there during prayer. My eyes almost always are lifted there during the Lord's Prayer, but it is during the Sacrament of the Eucharist when it is as if a magnet is drawing my eyes up. During the blessing of the bread and wine, I feel as if I am standing either at the foot of the cross or in the presence of the risen Lord. I have not tried it, but I don't believe it would be the same if my eyes were closed and I was looking at the blank insides of my eyelids. Of course my eyes are open when I pray as I do house work, peel potatoes, or, especially as I am driving the car. To do otherwise would be folly and could even be suicidal. Whether our eyes are open or closed doesn't seem to matter to God. I am sure he doesn't care. He only cares that we continue to pray.

Another body part I will speak of is the hands, just as in early childhood we were taught to kneel, we were also taught to fold our hands when we prayed. Today, with a few exceptions, most people still pray this way. I know my hands were always folded when I prayed until a few years ago when my pastor gave me a book to read. This was a book titled "With Open Hands". In it the author says that we all have secrets hidden deep in our hearts. They may be things we don't want to acknowledge, things we don't want others to know, but, most of all they may be things we are afraid to admit to God. Sometimes we hold things in that we are just not ready to bring to light. The author contends that when we pray with folded hands or with hands clasped tight together, we are holding on to these hidden things. It is when we open our hands that these secrets can be released. Since I read that book I find I cannot fold my hands as I pray, not that I am consciously hiding something, but in case there is something so hidden I have forgotten about it. Sometimes I merely place my hands with palms upwards in my lap and other times I place them open but together like the hands in the famous sculpture "The Praying Hands". I find I am comfortable with either position as long as they are opened.

One Sunday I noticed the minister had his hands open like a basket as he prayed. After service I asked him why he did this and he said he had been taught this method years ago. He went on to say he had been taught to place one hand palm upwards with the fingers curved and then place the other hand on top in the same position. The open hands will release all cares and concerns to God, and the cupped hands which form a kind of basket will hold any blessings coming from God. What a wonderful concept. I like it so much it is now what I do. Hands held in the lap, hands held like a basket, or hands held side by side like the sculpture; all these hands are held open. Is this really better than with the hands folded closed? Does it really matter? Of course not! It would not matter to God. He only wants us to pray.

Finally I will discuss the head. When we bow our heads in prayer, we are doing something very special; something that, in our country at least, has become almost a forgotten practice. In times past, when meeting someone, a man would remove his hat and bow, at least bow his head and a woman would curtsey. Today in Japan almost everyone bows when greeting another person as a sign of respect. In England, as in most monarchies, all must bow in the presence of the king or queen. Therefore, I say should we not bow, at least bow the head, when addressing the most Supreme Being of all? Other than being a sign of honor, of respect, and an acknowledgement of God's supremacy bowing the head can also serve another purpose. A sudden noise or movement can be distraction, and even closed eyes may pop open. If this should happen and your head is bowed, all you will see is whatever is below you. As I was taught in childhood, I still do bow my head while I am praying. The only exceptions are those mentioned previously. Then both my eyes and my head are raised up to the cross and now to the figure of Christ. Head bowed or raised? I am sure the love and respect in your heart and the words which are forthcoming from your lips are all that matter to God. He cares less how your head is held.

To go back to the beginning and the question asked there, the answer is NO......there is no proper position for prayer. Kneeling sitting, standing, or lying down are all fine. Eyes open or closed, hands opened or closed, head bowed or unbowed; all these are more or less dependent on the occasion and on your own personal preference. I am sure if we were able to ask God which he prefers, he would say that none of them matter just as long as we continue to talk with Him, as long as we continue to pray.

CHAPTER 2

NOW WHAT SHOULD I DO?

YOU ARE IN POSITION; KNEELING, sitting, standing, or even lying down. Now what should you do? Your parents taught you to fold your hands, close your eyes, and bow your head as you pray. In the previous chapter I discussed each of these things and the consensus I came to was that it is a personal decision. I have already covered the what's, the why's, the when's and the where's of prayer. Now is the time to get down to the nitty-gritty of prayer - the how.

Before I get serious, how about a bit of fancy on the subject of how to pray. Most of us have learned how to use voice mail. Have you ever wondered what it would be if God decided to install voice mail? Imagine you are beginning to pray when suddenly you hear the following: Thank you for calling heaven. For English press 1. For Spanish press 2. For all other languages press 3.please select one of the following options: Press 1 for requests. Press 2 for thanksgivings. Press 3 for complaints. Press 4 for all others. Oh. I am sorry but all our Angels and Saints are busy helping other sinners right now. However, your prayer is important to us and we will answer it in the order it was received. Please stay on the line. If you would like to speak to: God, press 1. To Jesus, press 2. The Holy Spirit, press 3. To find a loved one that you believe has been assigned to heaven, press 5, and then enter his social security number followed by the pound sign. If you receive a negative response, please hang up and dial area code 666. For reservations to heaven, please enter JOHN followed by the numbers 3 and 16. For answers to nagging questions, please wait until you arrive in heaven for the specifics. Our computers show that you have already been prayed for today, so please hang up and call again tomorrow. If you are calling after hours and need emergency assistance, please contact your local pastor. Thank you for calling and have a heavenly day. Of course this is pure fancy but I thought that at this point in the book, a bit of fancy would be good for the soul. And now, on to the real purpose of the book.

In Matthew 6:9, we are told that Jesus said: "Pray then in this way". This is followed by some of the most precious words we know, by the Lord's Prayer. Today these words are offered by churches and peoples world-wide. But, when Jesus gave us this prayer, He did not say only pray these words. I believe He did not mean this to be our only prayer; rather I believe He also gave it as an outline for our prayers. When we take a close look at the words, the outline becomes apparent. The opening words establish our relationship with God; they acknowledge His supremacy; they show His place; they proclaim His holiness. The following words show our hopes for eternal life with Him and our obedience to His will. Then come our requests; our wants, our needs, our desires for forgiveness for any wrong-doings. Finally come the closing words. Here we acknowledge His mighty power, power that created our world and all that is in it; we acknowledge His kingdom, and finally His glory that is eternal. If you think about it, isn't this the same form you use when writing a letter? You begin with a salutation or greeting, follow with whatever reason you are writing and then end it with some words of closure. Of course it is the same, since a letter is a communication with someone just as a prayer is communication with God.

Although Jesus gave us an outline for prayer, must we always follow it? If we use only a part or parts of it, is our prayer complete? Could even just a single word be a prayer? For example, when someone is deeply distressed, or in trouble and simply cries out the word "help", wouldn't He know the cry is being addressed to him since God knows our every thought? Therefore, wouldn't that single word be a prayer? If on occasion, a single word can be a prayer, what about a few words or a phrase? I will never forget the time when I kept repeating five words over and over. Those words: "Oh, God, I need you", came from the depth of my heart. They expressed a need I hadn't even known existed. God had to have heard them because from that moment on He entered my life and changed me forever. My heart had spoken and God had answered. These five words had to have been a prayer.

It may have happened, but I cannot remember a time when I started a prayer without addressing God by name, even if it was more of a conversation than a formal prayer. I recall that one day I came upon a yard filled with flowers of every possible hue. As I stood and admired this array of beauty, I recall I said something like: "God, you must have used all the colors on your palette for these flowers; you have created a lovely work of art". Another time I remember is a time when I had just arrived at our church camp in the north woods of Wisconsin. it was late in the day, the sun was about to disappear behind the hills and the whole scene was reflected in the lake before me. The last bit of brightness from the sun, the first colors of the sunset, the dark shape of the hills surrounded by dark green trees; all these presented a sight that was breathtaking in its beauty. I had no choice; I had to express my awe and gratitude to the creator of this glorious vision. As I recall, I fell to my knees as I said: "Oh Lord, I am in awe at what my eyes are beholding. I feel that you have sent a bit of heaven down to earth". These are just two examples I have given you. I could fill page after page recounting more, but I am sure they will prove my point. A few simple words or phrases can be a prayer.

What should I do now? Why not just open your lips and begin to sing? In Psalm 100:1-2. David tells us to: "Make a joyful noise unto the Lord, all the earth. Worship the Lord with gladness; come into His presence with singing". As we sing hymns in church we are voicing our concerns, our hopes, and our love to God; these are prayers. This is fine you say, but not all of us can sing. You may be like me and if I try to sing, even a bushel basket could not hold all the bad notes forth coming. But, I do sing; I sing when I am alone. When others are present I either mime or speak the words. There are some words I read once that I recall whenever I try to sing. They are: "You may think your singing voice is terrible, but

God thinks you are Caruso". So, even though it sounds discordant and awful to my ears, I do still sing knowing it sounds just fine to God.

You can speak your prayers, can sing your prayers, but you can also read them; read them in the Bible, especially in the book of Psalms. In the section on when to pray, I spoke of times of darkness; if this happens the words of Psalm 42 can help. If you speak foolish or thoughtless words which you later regret, the wonderful prayer in Psalm 39:1-9 will bring comfort and forgiveness. Living in today's world is not easy. There is little peace to be found anywhere; prices keep rising faster than wages; people are struggling to make ends meet; they are wishing there was help somewhere. But there is help available. When I am troubled I can always find help in the 23rd Psalm. Living in California, I can always find comfort and/or help in Psalm 121. Whatever you need, you can almost always find a Psalm to fit or fulfill it.

What should I do now? It matters not whether you think the words, speak them, sing them, or read them. The only thing that matters is that you do it; do it in communication with the Lord; do it in prayer.

CHAPTER 3

ALONE OR NOT ALONE?

ALONE OR NOT ALONE; THAT is the question. Must we follow Jesus' directive to go into a room alone to pray? Jesus himself wasn't always alone when he prayed, so why must we be? What are we to do; obey his words or follow his actions? Is this a case of "Do as I say and not as I do?" Or what is it? I feel the answer can be found in his earlier words in Matthew 6:1 and 6:5. In both cases He is warning us not to make a public showing of our piety. He says that those who do so are hypocrites, looking for admiration of their devoutness. But, this admiration will be their only reward; they will receive none from the Father.

Only once does the Bible tell of an incident when Jesus prayed so that He would be heard by a crowd. John II tells of the raising from the dead of Lazarus. When Jesus said: "Take away the stone", Martha protested and He said: "Did I not tell you that if you believed you would see the glory of God?" Then He looked upwards and prayed: "Father, I thank you for having heard me. I knew that you always hear me, but I have said this for the sake of the crowd standing here, so that they may believe that you sent me". This prayer was followed by His words: "Lazarus, come out". No, He wasn't being a hypocrite looking for admiration; He was establishing from whence came his power.

Of course Jesus would go off by himself to pray, but not always. The Bible recounts many times when others were present. When He asked God's blessing on the food about to be received at the feeding of the multitude and at the Last Supper, He was not alone. In essence He was asking the blessings on behalf of all those present. He was praying for them as well as for himself. We do the same when we say Grace before a family meal. Instead of each one praying, one person speaks for all. But, we can each make it our personal prayer by saying a solemn "Amen" at the close of the prayer. It is much the same at church suppers or other public meals. I think the best example would be the prayer blessing the bread and wine before its distribution during Holy Communion. In any case, one person asks the blessing for all those attending.

Meal time is not the only time we pray before others. During a church service there are the pastor's prayer and the prayer of dedication for the offering. In both cases the pastor prays for all those attending and again we can add the "Amen" to signify that it is our prayer also. We do not always sit silently while someone else prays on our behalf. Most obvious example is the Lord's Prayer. It is prayed in unison in Christian Churches world-wide as well as when opening classes or meetings.

Many denominations have prayers that they offer in unison. The Greek Orthodox Church is known for the

"Jesus Prayer" which is: "Lord Jesus Christ, Son of God, have mercy on me, a sinner". The Anglican Church has "The Book of Common Prayer". For centuries people around the world have used this book to pray the same prayer on the same day. Thus they are creating a world-wide unison of prayer. In some other churches such as the Nazarene, the Free Methodist, and the Wesleyan, their services consist mainly of songs of love, of devotion, and of praise. Of course, these songs sung in unison are prayers. Then, at times, after the service is ended, members will gather and pray together for a common concern. They will continue to pray until they feel God has responded. They call this "praying through" or "tarrying". But tarrying could not be only a Sunday after service practice. It could be in our daily lives as well. However, in today's hectic world, tarrying is fast becoming a lost art. People just do not seem to find the time to "tarry". However, time is available; just set the alarm ahead a bit or retire a bit earlier than usual and you will find the time. You do not always need a lot of time to pray. Psalm 34:15 tells us: "God's ears hear the cries of His people". In Isaiah 65:24 we are told: "Before they call I will answer, while they are still speaking I will hear". Of course God knows what we are about to say even before we say it. So, why not just tarry a while and see if He already has an answer for you?

These were examples of times for personal tarrying; there are also times for tarrying with others. Many believers form prayer groups. These groups meet together and pray together for common concerns. When they finish praying together, hopefully they will not just leave and go their separate ways, for this is the perfect time to tarry, to wait upon God. Far too often a pray-er does the praying and not the waiting.

What does it mean to wait on the Lord? The first thing needed is silence. Our voices need to be hushed and our minds and hearts need to be focused on God. We cannot hear a response if we are speaking and we will not sense His presence if our attention is elsewhere. The second thing needed is expectation. In Psalm 62:5, David says: "For God alone my soul waits in silence, for my hope is from Him". Unfortunately, most of us seem to expect the worst and not the good things that can and will come from God. Finally, we need to watch for a response. We must remain quiet enough and alert enough to feel His presence and to hear His voice. This is what is meant "To wait on the Lord".

Have you ever had a prayer partner or even considered the idea of one? I realize that many people's prayer requests are very personal and thus many people are hesitant, possibly ashamed or afraid to share them with others. But they need not be afraid or ashamed because their partner may also have similar personal matters and both will find that shared burdens will become lighter burdens; they will find strength in their shared prayers. You may wonder how to find a prayer partner. You realize you cannot just walk up to someone and ask them to be a partner. You understand it must be someone special. So, how do you find the right person?

Perhaps, if you are a member of a prayer group, over time you begin to feel a special closeness with someone. This person could very well become your prayer partner.

Perhaps you have been helping someone who is struggling with prayer. As their knowledge and ability grows, a feeling of closeness may develop and they may become your prayer partner. If you would really want a prayer partner, maybe the best way to find one would be to ask God for his help, and he will lead you to the very person you wished for.

The prayer chain is another means of praying with others. My church had such a chain. The only requirement to becoming a link is the have a computer and to promise to fill all requests in prayer. Only the person in charge knows who all the links are and he or she will e-mail each link a list of issues, concerns, and prayer requests from others. All requests are kept strictly confidential and are never spoken of to others. Even though we do not know the identities of the other links, we are prayer partners. A retreat is a wonderful place to go either with a prayer partner or to find a new one. What is meant by a retreat? As a verb the word retreat mans to withdraw and this is exactly what you must do; you must withdraw from the daily demands of your life. As a noun the word means a refuge, a place of privacy, a place of shelter from everyday life. So, basically a retreat is time spent with God where you won't be disturbed. Where should you go for a retreat? It doesn't really matter where you go as long as you are not disturbed and you feel comfortable there. How long should a retreat last? Some large group retreats may last for a week-end, a few of them may even last for a full week. Smaller groups, even just two or three believers may meet for a week-end, for a day, or maybe for just a part of a day such as from sunrise to sunset if circumstances dictate.

The length of time spent is not as important as the content and quality of the time spent, time spent with the Lord in prayer. Alone or not alone should no longer be a question. We can pray alone in privacy as Jesus said, or we can pray with others as Jesus did. It will make no difference to God, just as long as we spend that time in prayer.

CHAPTER 4

CENTERING PRAYER

HOPEFULLY, BY THIS TIME, MANY of you may have developed a personal prayer life or at least the beginnings of one. If not, if there are problems, if there seem to be things blocking the development of one, the I suggest before you read on, you go back and re-read any or all that I have written. As you do so, you may discover answers you missed the first time and the blockages could be lifted.

In this chapter I will be presenting what I feel in the next plateau in a prayer life. It is not a relaxation exercise; it is not self-hypnosis; it is not merely feeling the presence of God. It is the means to bring about a deeper relationship with God, a relationship which moves beyond conversation to communion.

The first step in achieving the centering prayer plateau is for each person to choose a personal "sacred word". This word is sacred, not because of its meaning, but rather because of its intent. It should express your intention to open to God. The word may be chosen during prayer, as the Holy Spirit stresses a word special to you. Once chosen, do not change the word; to do so would be to start thinking rather than feeling. Once the sacred word is selected, you should decide where and when to begin the prayer. Where is very important because it should be a place where you will be comfortable as well as a place that will offer the least chance of being disturbed. A noisy TV, a ringing phone, or even members of the family can make the needed concentration difficult to achieve and maintain. Perhaps this would be a time when Christ's words in Matthew 6:6, "Go into your room and shut the door" should be put to use.

When to begin is as important as where. Centering prayer is not something done in just a few minutes; it can and should last at least 20 to 30 minutes. Therefore, do not make a selection without sufficient time. If you have to be watching the clock, you will not be able to fully concentrate. Immediately after a meal is a poor time. Stop and think how often you have sat down and relaxed after a meal only to find you are drifting off to sleep. If this is the only time available, attempt to wait at least an hour or more before beginning. Neither is just before retiring a good time. In centering prayer all your senses reach a level unknown to you before, a level focused entirely on God. It can take several minutes or longer for them to return to normal, so to retire too soon after ending the prayer could make it difficult to sleep.

Ideally centering prayer should be attempted twice a day; the first thing in the morning and then in the afternoon or early evening would probably be best. However, all our daily lives are different; we all have obligations, but what time of day or night we fulfill them will vary. The schedules of everyone will be different from one another. However, any individual's may even be different from one day to another. Whatever time and location works on Monday through Friday may be entirely wrong on the weekend. Therefore, when and where you enter into a state of centering prayer has to be an individual decision, a decision which may have to be made each new day.

Now, you have selected your sacred word, you have selected a time when you won't have to be watching the clock. You are seated in a quiet, comfortable spot. Now, what do I do next, how do I begin, you wonder. What happens next is the beginning of an experience so unique, so awesome, that you will find you wish to repeat it soon.

To begin, make sure you are seated comfortably, and then close your eyes to shut out any possible distractions. Introduce your sacred word, then sit in complete silence and wait. It is at this point you may, and probably will, encounter problems. The level of consciousness required to achieve centering prayer does not come easily. It is human nature to react to sudden noises or movements and the ability to not even be aware of any and all disturbances can take time to develop. I know for me it was far from immediate; it didn't happen over night; it took me at least a couple of weeks.

If you have trouble even beginning, you could take time to first read some scripture; you could take a relaxing walk; or best of all, you could ask God's help to achieve the needed peace. Whatever you do, make sure that your thoughts and emotions are calm before starting. This is one reason why early in the day is a good time, since there will be fewer events yet to trouble you. One thing I hope you will not do is to become discouraged and give up trying. Finally you have reached the inner and outer peace and silence needed, so you wait.......wait for what comes next.

Centering prayer is reception, a reception of God's presence. We do not need to reach for Him, He is already present. Centering prayer is the movement of our developing relationship with God to the level of pure faith. Centering prayer is the raising of the mind and heart to God; but it is not we who do the lifting; that is the work of the Holy Spirit. The Holy Spirit will give our spirits rest and give us peace of mind. This will then become a seed bed for divine love to grow in. Centering prayer is not only the offering of our thoughts and acts to God, it is the offering of ourselves, of who and what we are.

One effect of centering prayer is a release of the unconscious; of things we may not even remember are hidden there or of things we may have wished to keep hidden, even from God. This release will bring about forgiveness and of course will bring peace to our souls. There are some things I feel I should mention here. As you near the level of centering prayer, you may feel a slight discomfort, may feel itches, or may feel twitches in various parts of your body. Just as a massage eases the tense muscles, these feelings are the work of the Holy Spirit untying any emotional knots it finds. Another thing that may happen is that something or someone may be successful in breaking into your concentration. Believe me, this can and probably will happen from time to time. If either happens, you can pay no attention, or you can merely rest briefly and then return to your sacred word, as this is the only action that will bring you back to where you were before the interruption.

How does a centering prayer end? Do you say "Amen" and then go about your normal daily life? Of course not! Just as it was God who brought you to this level of concentration, it is only God who can end it. All you need to do is to remain silent with your eyes closed for a few minutes. Then the Holy Spirit will gradually return your senses to normal.

Why am I placing so much emphasis on the importance of centering prayer you wonder? "After all," you say, "I have moved from the simple prayers of my youth to where I now find reasons and opportunities for prayer everywhere. Isn't that enough, or does God really want more?" Of course God will be happy if you never go beyond where you are now. He never tries to make us do something we are not ready to do. But, this does not mean that He doesn't hope that someday you will open yourself to the divine experience of centering prayer.

As I said earlier in this chapter, centering prayer is a unique and awesome experience, and anyone who attains this level will never again wonder why I place so much emphasis on it. Centering prayer will engender a new depth of feeling and love. You will reach a new level of faith. You will feel a lightness of spirit after receiving forgiveness for things hidden deep in your heart. Most important, although you have long felt God's presence in your life, that has changed. You have opened the innermost door and He has entered.

If you still have doubts, why not ask God for his opinion the next time you pray. Ask Him if centering prayer is really important, and then ask Him if he would wish you to participate. You will not see the word "yes" on the wall, but you will feel it in your heart. So, go ahead; give it a try!

CHAPTER 5

CONTEMPLATIVE PRAYER

IF YOU THOUGHT THAT CENTERING prayer was the final plateau in prayer, you were wrong. It is the necessary method designed to bring about contemplative prayer, the ultimate plateau in prayer.

Contemplative prayer can only be achieved when you have entered into centering prayer and are willing to go beyond. It is a journey into the unknown. It is a call to release all security blankets and practices we have used as props. Contemplative prayer is a call to forget self, forget the knowledge of whom and what we are, and to follow Jesus. In Matthew 16:24, Jesus says: "If any want to become my followers, let them deny themselves and take up their cross and follow me". persona; union with Christ as his follower is a path to divine union, and the love of God will take care of the rest of the journey. Everyone has the potential for divine union, but they must contend with human nature's tendency for evil. We all have the desire for more happiness, for more of God's love. But we must first dispel these evil tendencies.

The Holy Spirit will help and will remove any emotional junk. You need not try to separate or figure out where the junk came from. Like household garbage where you do not separate egg shells from orange peels, just lump it all together and let it go.

Contemplative prayer is pure solitude and this is not a place, it is an attitude of total commitment to God. It will open an awareness of God you never experienced before. You will know He is all around you, He is within you, He is never separate from you.

You have opened the door from within, now you must surrender yourself in silence and remain in openness to be loved. Let God's love take over and rest in his presence. God's presence is immense yet humble, awesome yet gentle, limitless yet tender and intimate and personal. He knows everything about you, all your weaknesses and sins, but He still loves you. His presence is healing, refreshing, and strengthening. It is not judgmental. You will feel as if you are returning to a place you should never have left. It is an awareness of something that had always been there, but you had not recognized it.

Tears may come during the prayer. They may express either joy or sorrow; they may also indicate the release of emotions that cannot be expressed in other ways. But, do not be troubled if this happens. Do not fight them; they are a gift from God.

Contemplative prayer's fruits are greater peace in our lives as well as greater humility and a deeper sense of charity. You will relate to others beyond social status, race, nationality, religion, or personal characteristics. We tend to think of prayer as thoughts or feelings expressed in words, but that is only one way. It can also be the laying of thoughts and feelings aside and the opening of the mind and heart, our whole being, to God. This is contemplative prayer. This is not just awareness of God's presence; this is divine union, a union initiated by God. We need only to surrender, surrender to be loved. This is contemplative prayer!

EPILOGUE

THERE IS ONLY ONE WAY to end this book; it must end with a prayer.

Heavenly Father: You are omnipotent, all powerful; you are omniscient, all knowing; you are omnipresent, always there for your people. You are the shepherd who leads me away from evil and guides me on the path to rightness and salvation; you are the rock on which I have built my life as your child.

With your omnipotence, Lord, you have filled my heart with love and joy; with your omniscience you have gifted me with your Holy Spirit to be my advocate. It was only through Him that I found the inspiration to begin this book and received the ability to complete it. I could never have done it alone.

Father, in your grace you have filled my life with gifts. In gratitude I present this book as a gift to you; a gift I pray will help the readers enhance their prayer lives; a gift I pray will draw them closer to you as they put into practice what they have learned. This is why I wrote this book; this is my prayer, a prayer offered in the name of your blessed Son and my beloved Redeemer Jesus.

Amen

Now it is your turn. Come on, don't hesitate, just speak up; God is waiting to hear from you!

ABOUT THE AUTHOR

D OROTHY IS A MOTHER OF three; grandmother of six, and great-grandmother of six.

She was born in Wisconsin, grew up in the Chicago area, lived for a while in the smog-filled Los Angeles area and then in coastal Maine. After retiring from the Postal Service, she moved to a small town in Wisconsin, and it was here that her life changed forever. During a Taize service, God entered her heart, and she became a true child of God.

In 2007, for health reasons, she moved to Santa Barbara, where she still resides filling her days with crafting, church activities, and fulfilling her call to share her gift from God—to write.